FROM BHARAT TO INDIA

FROM BHARAT TO INDIA

Naming Chronicles

MARIA M.

Spectra Enterprise

CONTENTS

INDEX

INTRODUCTION

The nomenclature of India is not an exception to the rule that the journey of a nation is typically mirrored in the name of the nation. Changing the name of the subcontinent from "Bharat" to "India" encapsulates a significant transformation that goes beyond semantics and delves into the fundamental identity, history, and aspirations of the subcontinent. An exploration of the cultural, political, and social factors that played a role in the evolution of the nation's name is the purpose of this naming chronicle, which is a trip through time.

This is the ancient heritage of Bharat.

The word "Bharat" originates from ancient Indian writings, most notably the Mahabharata, which is considered to be the most important of them. According to Hindu mythology, Bharat was a monarch who ruled in the past and was the son of monarch Dushyanta and Queen Shakuntala. Originally, the name "Bharatvarsha" was used to refer to the land that was under the dominion of King Bharat. However, it eventually came to be used to refer to the entire Indian subcontinent.

Over the course of several centuries, Bharat continued to serve as a representation of India's historical and cultural legacy. This was a term that was firmly ingrained in the customs and stories that characterized the subcontinent, and it helped to build a sense of oneness among the various communities that lived there.

Colonialism and the emergence of the continent known as "India"

It was during the colonial era that India's history underwent a critical turning point, and along with it came a change in the nomenclature of the country. The British East India Company, which was instrumental in the colonization of the subcontinent, coined the term "India" and made it widely known. The word "India" originates from the River Indus, which is located in the region's northwestern corner and is associated with the country.

When the British colonial influence spread, the term "India" began to be used to refer to the entire subcontinent. This trend continued till the present day. One of the goals of the colonial rulers was to establish a distinct geographical and administrative identity for the many regions that were under British control. The term "India" served as a unifying title for these territories.

The Struggle for Independence and the Significance of Names in Political Relationships

A rebirth of the term "Bharat" as a symbol of struggle against colonial control occurred during the decades of the 20th century, when India was fighting for its freedom.

Leaders such as Mahatma Gandhi and Subhas Chandra Bose frequently referred to the nation as "Bharat," thereby invoking the nation's historical and cultural origins in order to rally the masses.

An important factor that contributed to the formation of the nomenclature issue was the political environment. There were talks that took place over the post-independence name for the nation as the drive for self-rule gathered strength after independence. In the course of deliberations on this subject, the Constituent Assembly of India considered the historical significance of the term "Bharat" in comparison to the administrative convenience and international acceptance that are connected with the term "India."

Bharat and India: Comparing Their Constitutional Options

It was ultimately decided by the people who drafted the Indian Constitution that a dual nomenclature would be used. This decision was made in recognition of the historical and cultural significance of both "Bharat" and "India." In the first article of the Constitution, it is stated that "India, which is also known as Bharat, shall be a Union of States." The dual nomenclature of a nation that is situated at the intersection of tradition and modernity is a reflection of the dual identity of that nation.

Although the name "India" is the one that is most commonly used around the world, the word "Bharat" serves as a reminder of the nation's rich cultural legacy and cultural diversity. A constitutional compromise is being proposed with the intention of bringing the historical legacy into harmony with the modern global situation.

The rich tapestry of names that represents cultural and linguistic diversity

The nation of India is a patchwork of languages, each of which has contributed its own name to the country. In Hindi, which is the official language of the government of India, the nation is referred to as "Bharat." Nevertheless, in other languages such as Tamil, it is referred to as "◇◇◇◇◇◇◇" (Indiyā), and in Bengali, it is referred to as "◇◇◇◇" (Bhārort). The intricacy of India's identity and the myriad of ways in which it is viewed are further highlighted by the country's linguistic diversity.

Bharat versus India: A Comparison of Contemporary Perspectives

When it comes to current speech, the decision between "Bharat" and "India" frequently reflects the ideological and political affinities of the respective parties. There are many who advocate for the exclusive usage of the term "Bharat" because they believe it to be a symbol of cultural pride and historical continuity. In contrast, those who advocate for the term "India" claim that it should be recognized internationally and should have relevance in the modern world.

Beyond the realm of linguistics, the dispute over name touches upon issues pertaining to identity, nationality, and the vision for the future. This is a highly sophisticated conversation that sheds light on the continuing struggle that takes place between legacy and globalization, as well as tradition and progress.

Communication and Diplomacy on a Global Scale

Within the context of the global community, the term "India" has come to be synonymous with a nation that is fast developing and that is a center of democracy, culture, and technology. "India" is a brand that has a value that goes beyond its borders, which is significant from an economic point of view. The selection of a name is not only a matter of personal preference in terms of language; rather, it is a strategic decision that has implications for diplomatic ties, trade alliances, and the perception of the world.

How to Move Forward: Finding Your Way Through Identity in the 21st Century

The dual nomenclature is a reflection of the delicate balance that India strives to preserve as it moves forward into the 21st century. An appreciation of the vast tapestry of history, culture, and variety that constitutes the subcontinent is what this statement is.

The ongoing argument between "Bharat" and "India" is a microcosm of the wider conversation about identity and nationhood in a world that is becoming increasingly interconnected. In the process of recognizing its roots, it encourages introspection into the manner in which a nation defines itself in relation to the global setting.

The voyage of India's name is a monument to the nation's tenacity, adaptability, and complexity. From the ancient echoes of "Bharat" in the epics to the colonial imprint of "India" and the constitutional compromise of dual nomenclature, the transformation of India's name is a fascinating and fascinating journey. The book "From Bharat to India: Naming Chronicles" is not just a linguistic investigation; rather, it is a voyage through time, culture, politics, and identity. It captures the essence of a nation that straddles the line between tradition and modernity. As India continues to develop, the names it chooses to use will also continue to change. This is because India is a nation that resists easy categorization, and its narrative tends to change over time.

Chapter 1

Introduction

The change from "Bharat" to "India" is more than a shift in nomenclature; it is a trip through the cultural, historical, and political tapestry of the Indian subcontinent. The book "From Bharat to India: Naming Chronicles" is an investigation of this process that delves into the complexities of names and the deep consequences that they have on the identity of a nation. Ancient mythology, colonial legacies, wars for independence, constitutional considerations, linguistic diversity, and contemporary perspectives are all included in this voyage, which reveals the diverse essence of a nation that straddles the line between tradition and modernity.

There are remnants of ancient heritage in Bharat

In the epic Mahabharata, the name "Bharat" may be traced back to its roots, which are resonant with the echoes of old Indian tradition. The word "Bharatvarsha" came to be used to refer to the entire Indian subcontinent as a result of the legendary king Bharat's dominion over a broad territory. With its origins in Hindu mythology, the term "Bharat" evolved into a unifying force, symbolizing the diverse cultural and historical fabric that has defined the subcontinent for ages.

This section explores the cultural significance of the name "Bharat" as a name that encompasses a wide range of communities and brings them together under a common historical narrative. A sense of oneness among the people of the subcontinent is fostered as a result of this exploration of the mythical origins of the phrase as well as the process by which it became embedded in the collective consciousness.

Colonialism and the emergence of the continent known as "India"

Because of the significant part that the British East India Company had in defining the identity of the region, the colonial era was accompanied by a seismic upheaval in the nomenclature of the people who lived there. There is a toponymic connection to the River Indus, which flowed through the northern parts of the subcontinent, which is where the term "India" originated. Throughout the course of the expansion of British colonial rule, the term "India" eventually evolved into the umbrella term for the various areas that were under British administration.

The colonial influence on the naming of the subcontinent is dissected in this section, which also investigates the manner in which the British East India Company made strategic use of the word "India" in an effort to establish a distinct administrative and geographical identity.

The repercussions of this renaming on the political and cultural landscape of the subcontinent are investigated in depth in this article.

"Bharat" as a Symbol of Resistance During the Struggle for Independence for India

A rebirth of the term "Bharat" as a symbol of resistance against colonial control occurred during the battle for independence that took place in the 20th century across India. The historical and cultural connotations of the word "Bharat" were used by visionary leaders such as Mahatma Gandhi and Subhas Chandra Bose in order to galvanize the masses. During the time of the independence movement, this part investigates how the desire for self-rule rekindled the cultural meaning of the term "Bharat" and how it played a role in molding the nationalistic fervor that was there.

In the discussion of naming, the political climate that prevailed throughout this time period was an extremely important factor. As the leaders of the nation struggled to choose what the nation should be called after it gained its independence, the importance of the word "Bharat" became the focal point of their discussion. A number of discussions took place within the Constituent Assembly of India, during which the historical and cultural significance of the term "Bharat" was evaluated against the administrative ease and international recognition that are connected with the term "India."

Considerations Regarding the Constitution: "Bharat" and "India" in Congruence

In the end, the people who drafted the Constitution of India decided to use a dual nomenclature because they acknowledged the historical and cultural significance of both "Bharat" and "India." It is stated in Article 1 of the Constitution that "India, that is Bharat, shall be a Union of States." The dual character of a nation that is at the crossroads of tradition and modernity is reflected in this constitutional compromise.

The ramifications of adopting both names on the identity of the nation are discussed in this section, along with the constitutional intricacies that are involved in doing so. This article dives into the arguments that took place within the Constituent Assembly as well as the rationale behind the decision to accept both "Bharat" and "India" as official names for the republic.

The rich tapestry of names that represents cultural and linguistic diversity

India is a nation that is rich in linguistic diversity, and each of the linguistic communities that make up India has contributed their own name to the country. Bharat is the name that is used to refer to the nation in Hindi, which is the official language of India. However, other languages have their own names for the nation. In this section, we investigate the linguistic diversity that exists in the process of naming the nation.

Specifically, we investigate how many languages capture the spirit of India through their own unique linguistic subtleties.

The fact that the country is known by a number of different names is not only a matter of linguistic curiosity; rather, it is a manifestation of the diverse array of cultures and languages that comprise the Indian subcontinent. The purpose of this study is to analyze the ways in which these various names contribute to the varied identity of Canada.

In the 21st century, "Bharat" and "India" are viewed from different contemporary perspectives

The choice between "Bharat" and "India" in contemporary discourse goes beyond individuals' preferences on the language they use. It turns into a reflection of the political and ideological affinities of the individual. The purpose of this section is to examine the ongoing controversy that surrounds the use of the terms "Bharat" and "India" in the modern context. Specifically, this section will investigate how various points of view create the narrative of the nation.

The discussion on the naming of the property is not limited to semantics; rather, it touches upon more general questions concerning identity, nationalism, and the vision for the future. As India navigates the problems and opportunities of the 21st century, the decision between "Bharat" and "India" becomes emblematic of the continuing conflict between tradition and progress, heritage and globalization. "Bharat" is not the same thing as "India."

A Look at the Influence of Names on International Relations and Diplomacy

On a worldwide scale, the term "India" has come to be synonymous with a nation that is fast developing and a global player in the fields of technology, culture, and democracy. This section examines the influence that names have on the attitudes of people all across the world, as well as on diplomatic ties and commercial collaborations. It investigates the ways in which the decision between "Bharat" and "India" affects India's position on the worldwide arena and has an effect on the narrative that is told about India in the international community.

The choice of a name is not merely a matter of personal preference in terms of language; rather, it is a strategic decision that has repercussions for diplomatic engagements, trade alliances, and global recognition. In order to comprehend India's role in the international arena, it is essential to have a solid understanding of this dynamic.

How to Move Forward: Finding Your Way Through Identity in the 21st Century

In the midst of India's transition into the 21st century, the dual nomenclature of "Bharat" and "India" encapsulates the complicated dance that the nation performs between its traditional values and its contemporary values. The ramifications of the naming chronicles for India's future are discussed in this particular segment, which is the concluding one. This article investigates the ways in which the nation embraces the challenges and opportunities presented by a rapidly changing global scene while also grappling with its historical foundations.

The discussion that always takes place between "Bharat" and "India" is not a static conversation but rather an ever-evolving dialogue that reflects the journey that the nation has taken. In a world in which identities are becoming more malleable and the borders between tradition and development are always being renegotiated, it provokes inquiry into the manner in which a nation defines itself.

A voyage through time, culture, politics, and identity, "From Bharat to India: Naming Chronicles" is a trip that unravels the threads that weave the narrative of a nation using the strands that are woven together. There is more to the change from "Bharat" to "India" than just a language evolution; it is also a reflection of the intricate strata that make up the Indian subcontinent. The name chronicle captures the character of a nation that resists easy categorization, from the ancient echoes of "Bharat" in the epics to the colonial stamp of "India" and the constitutional compromise of dual nomenclature. All of these elements contribute to the naming chronicle.

India is continuing its journey into the 21st century, and the names it chooses to use will continue to have an impact on the narrative it chooses to tell. Rather from being two distinct identities that compete with one another, "Bharat" and "India" are complementing aspects of a nation that takes strength from its history while simultaneously managing the difficulties and opportunities of the present and the future. It is a monument to the resiliency, adaptability, and enduring spirit of a nation that continues to be, at its core, a kaleidoscope of varied identities unified under the vast umbrella of its nomenclature that the naming chronicles of India are a testament to.

1.1 Overview of the importance of names in shaping national identity

There is a significant significance that names hold in the process of forming the identities of nations. In addition to being merely linguistic labels, they are indicative of the history, culture, aspirations, and collective consciousness of a country. There is a close connection between the process of naming a nation and the construction of its identity. This connection has an impact on how the nation perceives itself as well as how the world perceives it. In this essay, we investigate the varied function that names have in the formation of national identity. We look at the historical, cultural, linguistic, and political aspects of this significance.

Analyzing the Development of Nationhood Through Names: An Examination of Historical Roots

In many cases, the voyage of a nation starts with the naming of the nation, which signifies the nation's very first appearance on the historical stage. These names are not chosen at random; rather, they bear the weight of historical histories, capturing the challenges, successes, and milestones that define the course of a nation. For instance, the United States of America gets its name from the union of individual states, which is a reflection of the federal structure that is ingrained in the nation's character.

The purpose of this section is to investigate the ways in which historical circumstances have an impact on the naming process and the ways in which nations manifest a sense of continuity or rupture with the past through their names. There is a connection between the present and the collective memory of a nation that is established by the historical origins that are embedded in names.

Names as cultural artifacts: They carry significant cultural meaning

When it comes to a nation's cultural identity, names are cultural artifacts that encode the essence of that culture. The language traditions, mythology, folklore, and shared symbols that resonate with the cultural fabric of the society are frequently the sources from which they take inspiration at times. In the context of India, for example, the term "Bharat" brings with it rich cultural and historical meanings that have their origins in ancient mythology and epics.

The purpose of this section is to investigate the process by which names become stores of cultural values and ideas. This article examines the symbolic significance of names in terms of how they reflect the distinctive qualities, customs, and values of a nation. Names, in their capacity as cultural markers, play a role in the formation of a collective identity with the purpose of bringing together various communities within the context of a national framework.

Names as Expressions of Multilingual Narratives: Understanding the Role of Linguistic Diversity

Countries frequently boast of their linguistic diversity, and the selection of a name becomes a sensitive negotiation of the identities of the languages spoken by the people. In multilingual countries such as India, where a large number of languages coexist, it might be difficult to select a name that is able to resonate across linguistic boundaries. The persistence of names such as "Bharat" and "India" within the setting of India is a reflection of the linguistic diversity that exists inside the country.

This part of the article investigates the ways in which names might serve as linguistic bridges, bringing together various linguistic communities under a single national banner. This study investigates the many approaches that nations take to address the issue of linguistic variety in naming, taking into account the numerous voices and expressions that exist inside their borders.

The importance of names as instruments of power and legitimacy in political dynamics

The naming of nations is frequently a political act that is used as a tool to exercise power, legitimacy, and authority. It is possible for governments to employ names in a strategic manner in order to bolster political ideology, make territorial claims, or express a break from historical legacies.

One prominent example of this political dimension is the renaming of countries or towns, which is a form of political maneuvering in which politicians attempt to rewrite narratives and redefine national identities.

This section investigates the political dynamics of naming, focusing on the ways in which leaders utilize names in order to consolidate power, legitimize governance, or promote particular ideological objectives. This paper investigates the arguments and controversies that frequently accompany political decisions pertaining to naming, as well as the ramifications these decisions have for the unity or division of the nation.

The Role of Branding in the International Arena Through the Lens of Global Perceptions

Across the world, people's impressions of nations are significantly influenced by their names. On the global arena, they serve as tools for branding that communicate a nation's image, beliefs, and goals to the rest of the world. The decision of whether to use native names or anglicized versions of Native American names is a reflection of a nation's place within the international community. In 1989, Myanmar underwent a transition from Burma to Myanmar, which was accompanied by political and diplomatic reforms. These shifts signaled a departure from Myanmar's colonial heritage.

The purpose of this section is to investigate the role that names play as representatives of national identity, contributing to the way in which nations are seen by the worldwide community. The interconnectivity of national and international identities is brought to light through the analysis of the strategic factors that constitute the basis for decisions about names in the global arena.

The Role of Names in Fostering Social Cohesion in Societies That Are Diverse

When it comes to creating social cohesiveness in various communities, names play a very important role. They serve as components that bring people together, regardless of those differences being geographical, racial, or religious. Citizens are more likely to feel like they belong to a nation when they have a common national name that serves as a rallying point. In the opposite direction, the lack of a consensus on a national name may make existing social divisions even more pronounced.

In the following section, we will investigate the ways in which names contribute to social cohesion and the creation of nations. Specifically, we will investigate situations in which the selection of a name has either helped to alleviate or exacerbate internal tensions. Specifically, it explores the delicate balance that must be maintained between recognizing variety and cultivating a cohesive national identity through the use of a common name.

In a world that is constantly evolving, contemporary challenges include reevaluating names.

In the modern world, states are struggling to overcome the obstacles posed by changing identities, globalization, and shifting geopolitical landscapes. Names that were originally thought to be unchangeable and unchanging may come under review as cultures reevaluate the historical narratives and cultural values that they have established themselves. It is possible that nations will rethink names that bear colonial histories or exclude specific people in response to questions of decolonization, representation, and inclusivity.

In the following section, we will investigate the present difficulties that nations confront while attempting to navigate the complexity of identity through names. In this article, we examine several instances of name changes, disputes, and reforms that are reflective of the dynamic character of national identity in a world that is constantly changing.

The phenomena of the significance of names in the formation of national identity is one that is both dynamic and varied. The complicated fabric of a nation's identity is woven together by its names, which encompass every aspect of a nation's identity, from its historical roots and cultural significance to its linguistic diversity, political dynamics, global perceptions, social cohesiveness, and modern issues. Naming is not a static act but rather an ongoing discourse that reflects the developing narratives, goals, and problems of a society. This dialogue is reflected in the process of naming objects.

When it comes to recognizing the complexity of nationhood in a globalized world, it is essential to have a solid understanding of the function that names play in the construction of identities. Names are not only labels; rather, they are manifestations of collective consciousness that encapsulate the rich tapestry of history, culture, and aspirations that characterize a nation. Names are not simply labels. In the process of nations continuing to struggle with their identities, names will continue to be at the forefront of this continuous narrative, and they will continue to shape the contours of national identity for decades coming forward.

1.2 Brief historical context of the Indian subcontinent

Over the course of thousands of years, the Indian subcontinent, which is located in South Asia and is a huge and diverse region, has a history that is both rich and complex. From the Indus Valley's ancient civilizations to the arrival of colonial control and the following fight for independence, the history of the Indian subcontinent is characterized by a rich tapestry of cultures, empires, and sociopolitical developments. This can be seen from the beginning of the subcontinent's history to the present day. This article offers a concise historical framework, chronicling the significant epochs that have played a significant role in transforming the region into the multifaceted and vibrant subcontinent that we are familiar with today.

Civilizations from the past, including the Harappan and Vedic periods

In the Indian subcontinent, there is evidence of one of the world's first civilizations, the Indus Valley Civilization, which dates back to ancient times. The history of the Indian subcontinent goes back to ancient times. The towns of Mohenjo-Daro and Harappa flourished between the years 3300 and 1300 BCE. They were sites of complex urban design, sophisticated drainage systems, and a script that has not been deciphered to this day. The civilization that flourished in the Indus Valley is a living testimony to the advanced and ancient cultural advances that occurred in the region.

Following the collapse of the civilization that flourished in the Indus Valley, the Vedic period witnessed the writing of the sacred scriptures that are collectively referred to as the Vedas. During their migration to the subcontinent, the Indo-Aryans set the groundwork for the Vedic civilization. They had a significant impact on the religious and social activities that would later form an essential part of the region's cultural fabric.

The Mauryan and Gupta Empires: The Age of Classical

The establishment of major empires on the Indian subcontinent occurred during the classical age, with the Maurya and Gupta Empires being particularly notable. The

Mauryan Empire, which lasted from 322 BCE to 185 BCE, expanded its dominion throughout a significant portion of the subcontinent while Chandragupta Maurya and Ashoka were responsible for its expansion. Among the many things that people remember about Ashoka is his conversion to Buddhism, as well as his dedication to nonviolence and religious tolerance.

The Gupta Empire, which lasted from 320 to 550 CE, is frequently understood to be the "Golden Age" of Indian history. This time period was characterized by a flourishing of the arts, literature, and sciences, as evidenced by the accomplishments in the fields of mathematics and astronomy, as well as the production of fine sculptures and paintings. The Gupta era is seen as a period of intellectual and cultural flourishing, and it is revered for this.

Cultural flourishings and dynasties that existed during the Middle Ages

In the Indian subcontinent, the medieval period was characterized by the rise and fall of a number of different kingdoms, as well as the beginning and end of a number of cultural and artistic traditions. In the south, the Rashtrakuta, Chola, and Vijayanagara Empires played a significant influence in establishing the socio-political environment. In the north, the Delhi Sultanate and, subsequently, the Mughal Empire made significant contributions to the formation of the terrain.

The Delhi Sultanate, which lasted from 1206 to 1526, was the organization that initiated Muslim sovereignty in certain regions of northern India.

The Mughal Empire, which was established by Babur and lasted from 1526 until 1857, was a time of great creative and architectural accomplishments, particularly during the reigns of Akbar, Shah Jahan, and Aurangzeb. One of the most enduring symbols of this time period is the Taj Mahal, which is considered to be a masterpiece of Mughal construction.

Colonial Era: The Struggle for Independence and the Rule of the British

An important turning point in the history of the Indian subcontinent was the beginning of European powers' colonization of the region. Over the course of the 17th century, the British East India Company established its foothold in the region, steadily growing its influence through commerce and diplomatic practices. Beginning in earnest in the middle of the 18th century, the colonial era began, and by the middle of the 19th century, the British Crown had gained direct rule over India.

One of the most significant economic improvements that occurred during British control was the establishment of a unified legal system, as well as the introduction of railways and the telegraph. On the other hand, it resulted in the exploitation of resources, the inequality of economic conditions, and the disruption of cultural norms. The Indian independence movement began in the 19th and 20th centuries, with prominent people such as Mahatma Gandhi, Jawaharlal Nehru, and Subhas Chandra Bose serving as its leaders.

Civil disobedience, nonviolent protests, and mass movements were all prominent components of India's war for independence, which ultimately resulted in the country's attainment of independence in 1947. One of the most significant events in the history of the subcontinent is the partitioning of the subcontinent into India and Pakistan, which was accompanied by sectarian bloodshed and enormous migrations.

Construction of the Nation and Economic Development in the Post-Independence Era

In the years immediately following independence, the Indian subcontinent was confronted with the tremendous challenge of constructing a functional nation. A democratic political system was implemented in India, and the country's leaders made efforts to solve concerns relating to social justice, education, and poverty respectively. It was in the early 1990s when the nation began implementing economic changes, which marked the beginning of a period of liberalization and globalization.

When it came to handling various people, language and cultural divides, and territorial issues, India, along with Pakistan and subsequently Bangladesh, faced a number of obstacles. A geopolitical facet was added to the history of the region as a result of the nuclearization of the region. The subcontinent has made great progress in terms of economic development, technical improvements, and worldwide impact, despite the hurdles that it has faced.

Current Dynamics: Obstacles and Opportunities in the Contemporary World

In the present day, the dynamics of the Indian subcontinent show a territory that is in a state of change, attempting to strike a balance between ancient customs and contemporary goals. There are a number of factors that contribute to the subcontinent's global prominence, including rapid urbanization, technological breakthroughs, and a vastly increasing youth population. Despite this, the region continues to struggle with significant socioeconomic inequality, environmental issues, and political complications.

A focal point of regional dynamics continues to be the relationship between India and Pakistan, which has been molded by historical animosities between the two countries. Existing geopolitical tensions are exacerbated by a number of factors, including the conflict in Kashmir, territorial disputes, and the danger of terrorism. Following the country's attainment of independence in 1971, Bangladesh has made great advancements in both its economic and social development.

In the fabric of the Subcontinent, cultural diversity is the fabric

One of the characteristics that distinguishes the Indian subcontinent is the cultural diversity that it possesses. The cultural fabric of the region is a mosaic of customs, festivals, art forms, and gastronomic pleasures. This is due to the fact that the region is home to a large number of languages, religions, and ethnic groups. The cultural expressions of the subcontinent, which include the traditional dance styles of Bharatanatyam and Kathak as well as the lively celebrations of Diwali and Holi, are a reflection of the diversity that is present in the region.

The region's cultural vitality is enhanced by the region's extensive literary tradition, which includes works by contemporary authors such as Rabindranath Tagore and Arundhati Roy as well as ancient epics such as the Mahabharata and the Ramayana. The cultural relevance of the subcontinent is further highlighted by the fact that

Bollywood, which is also a global phenomenon, has had a significant impact on the film industry.

There is a story of perseverance, diversity, and ongoing change that can be found in the historical setting of the Indian subcontinent. Complex historical currents have been navigated by the subcontinent throughout its history, from the emergence of ancient civilizations to the rise of medieval empires, from the difficulties of colonial authority to the victories of freedom. The history of this region is a demonstration of the resilience of cultural traditions, the dynamism of political systems, and the adaptation of societies in the face of change.

As the Indian subcontinent continues to advance, it is coming to terms with the problems of the modern day while also drawing into the wealth of its history.

It is not a static account of the region's history; rather, it is a dynamic narrative that is influenced by the continual contributions of its people, the complexities of its geopolitical interactions, and the ambitions of its different communities. To fully appreciate the complexities of the Indian subcontinent and its place in the international community, it is necessary to have a solid understanding of the historical framework it exists within.

1.3 Introduction to the evolution of the name "India" from ancient times

Throughout the course of millennia, the name "India" has been associated with a diverse range of historical, cultural, and geographical implications that have developed throughout time. The trip of this appellation is not only a manifestation of linguistic change; rather, it is a reflection of the myriad of influences that have contributed to the formation of the identity of the Indian subcontinent. The evolution of the word "India" is a nuanced investigation of the complicated narrative of the subcontinent, beginning with its ancient roots in Sanskrit scriptures and continuing through its acceptance by colonial powers and its subsequent importance in the post-independence era.

Found in Sanskrit texts are the ancient languages of Bharat and Sindhu

It is possible to trace the origins of the name "India" all the way back to the ancient Sanskrit manuscripts that serve as the foundation of Indian traditions and philosophical thought. The term "Bharat" receives a significant amount of attention in these works, and its origins can be traced back to the mythical figure of King Bharata from Hindu mythology. It was the land that King Bharata controlled that became known as "Bharatvarsha," and it came to represent the Indian subcontinent.

It is also important to note that the term "Sindhu" is an additional ancient name that carries significance. The term "Sindhu" was derived from the Sanskrit word for river, and it was used to refer to the powerful Indus River, which ran across the northwest part of the subcontinent. After the Greeks, who had seen this region during their conquests, changed the phrase to "Indos," and it was from this that the name "India" subsequently evolved in Western languages.

The appearance of "India" in the Western world can be traced back to the Greek and Roman encounters

Interactions between the Greek and Indian civilizations took place during the Hellenistic period. Alexander the Great's wars were responsible for bringing the Indian subcontinent to the attention of the Western world. It was in Greek literature, such as those of Herodotus and Megasthenes, that the term "Indos" or "Indoi" was used to describe the geography, customs, and richness of the area that lay beyond the Indus River.

The Romans, who were influenced by Greek stories, continued to spread the word "India" throughout their works on the subject. Ptolemy and Pliny the Elder were among the individuals who contributed to the propagation of the word, which ultimately resulted in the establishment of the name as a recognizable identifier for the vast and unknown continent to the east.

From the Perspective of the Middle Ages: Arab Merchants and European Travelers

It was during the medieval period that Arab merchants and travelers played a significant part in the perpetuation of the name "India" through their interactions with the subcontinent. "Al-Hind" is a name that originated in Arabic and eventually became a frequent appellation for the Indian subcontinent in Islamic scriptures. This name, which is derived from the word "Sindhu," was popularized even further by Arab geography academics and geographers.

During the medieval period, European travelers and explorers, like Marco Polo, continued to make references to "India" in their writings. As a result of the Silk Road and other marine trade routes, cultural interactions were made easier, and the label "India" became firmly established in the minds of Europeans all across the world.

Colonial Period: The Establishment of "India" as a Governing Body Under British Control

The period of colonial rule was a period of profound change in the history of the Indian subcontinent, not only in terms of politics and economics but also in terms of language. As a result of the fast expansion of the British East India Company's power, the name "India" became a simple and unifying title for the enormous areas that were under British authority.

Alongside the consolidation of British power came the standardization of geographical designations, administrative changes, and the formation of a colonial identity. All of these events occurred simultaneously. The term "India" was used not only in official documents and maps, but also in literature, which further solidified its position as the primary identifier for the subcontinent.

Considerations Regarding the Constitution: "India" and "Bharat" in the Post-Independence Epoch

During the middle of the 20th century, while the nation was fighting for its independence, the titles that were used for the nation were reevaluated. Taking into consideration the historical and cultural significance of the term "Bharat," the leaders of the independence movement pondered on the nomenclature that would be used once the country gained its freedom.

A dual nomenclature was ultimately chosen by the individuals who were responsible for drafting the Indian Constitution.

In the first article of the Constitution, it is stated that "India, which is also known as Bharat, shall be a Union of States." This constitutional compromise aimed to acknowledge both the historical and cultural origins of the term "Bharat" as well as the international recognition that is closely associated with the term "India."

"India" in the Context of the World Today: Contemporary Utilisation

India is a nation that is fast developing and plays a key role on the global scene. In the modern era, the name "India" has become synonymous with this nation. The term is utilized in the context of international trade, cultural exchanges, and diplomatic relations. Both the information age and globalization have contributed to the further consolidation of the word "India" as the official name of the nation on a worldwide scale.

This dual identity of a nation that attempts to integrate its historic legacy with the needs of the modern world is shown in the coexistence of "Bharat" in the framework of India, despite the fact that "India" continues to be the designation that is recognized worldwide.

A fascinating voyage that highlights the intersections of history, culture, and linguistic traditions, the history of the word "India" from ancient times to the present day is a fascinating adventure. From its origins in Sanskrit writings and ancient Greek and Roman contacts to its consolidation under British colonial authority and its post-independence dual nomenclature, the name "India" encompasses the various influences that have contributed to the formation of the identity of the subcontinent.

It is a tribute to the delicate debate that takes place between tradition and modernity that the terms "Bharat" and "India" coexist in the contemporary environment. Not only does the name "India" continue to represent a geopolitical entity, but it also continues to represent a vibrant and dynamic civilization that has a rich historical history. This is true even as the nation moves forward into the future. The development of this name is a reflection of the complicated history of a nation that, despite its rise to prominence on the international stage, continues to be deeply rooted in its ancient past.

Chapter 2

Ancient Roots: Bharat and Beyond

It is the term "Bharat" that brings with it the echoes of ancient heritage, which is profoundly ingrained in the cultural, historical, and mythical tapestry of the Indian subcontinent. Its origins can be traced back to the sacred writings of ancient India, where it was found to have resonance as a symbol of unity, identity, and the continuation of civilization. This investigation into the ancient origins of the word "Bharat" goes beyond linguistic intricacies and delves into the mythological narratives, historical underpinnings, and cultural significance that have bestowed upon it a legacy that is both timeless and enduring.

Bharata in Hindu Epics: The Mythological Foundations of the Idea

The origins of the term "Bharat" can be traced back to the vast regions of Hindu mythology, where it is intricately connected to the epic stories of the Mahabharata and the Ramayana. In the epic known as the Mahabharata, the name Bharat is more than just a name; it is the name of a legendary ruler whose dynasty was responsible for shaping the destiny of the subcontinent.

According to the Mahabharata, King Bharata was the son of Dushyanta and Shakuntala. His reign is revered as a time of prosperity and morality, and it is a period that is honored. The story of Bharata's ancestry is an important component of cultural memory, serving as a representation of the principles of dharma (righteousness) and the obligations that come with being a monarch.

In a similar vein, Bharata is an important figure in the legendary Ramayana. The fact that he is Lord Rama's younger brother and that he refuses to ascend to the throne in the absence of Rama, who is currently living in exile, is one of the most important aspects of the epic. Bharata's steadfast devotion to his brother and his dedication to dharma are two examples that highlight the moral and ethical values that are ingrained in the ancient Indian system of thought.

When it comes to history, Bharatvarsha and the ancient territories are both significant.

Beyond the sphere of mythology, the term "Bharat" came to be synonymous with the geographical expanse that accounts for the Indian subcontinent. The name "Bharatvarsha" is used to refer to the region that was ruled by King Bharata. This phrase is recorded in ancient books such as the Puranas. By virtue of this territorial link, the word "Bharat" was elevated from the realm of mythology to that of a concrete geographical identity.

According to the Puranas, Bharatvarsha is a region that is characterized by its sacred rivers, unique ecosystems, and thriving local cultures. From the eastern to the western oceans, the ancients conceived of Bharatvarsha as the area that was situated between the Himalayas in the country's northernmost region and the Indian Ocean in its southernmost region. The notion of "Bharat" as a cultural and territorial entity was established on the basis of this geographical understanding, which set the building blocks.

Bharat, as a unifying force, holds significant cultural significance

Beyond its historical and mythological roots, the cultural significance of the word "Bharat" extends far beyond those factors. The different linguistic, ethnic, and religious communities that make up the Indian subcontinent have been brought together by it, serving as a unifying factor that has brought them together. The phrase encapsulates the shared heritage, values, and customs that have developed over the course of millennia.

The idea of "Bharat" as a cultural entity can be seen mirrored in historical works of art, literary works, and philosophical discourse. Bharatvarsha is envisioned as the sacred venue for the expression of arts and culture in the Natya Shastra, which is an ancient treatise on performing arts. A significant source of inspiration for the classical dance forms, music, and literature that have flourished in the region is the cultural ethos that is entrenched in the concept of "Bharat."

literary works and poetic expressions written in Sanskrit

Literature written in Sanskrit has been an essential component in the process of expressing the cultural and historical importance of the term "Bharat." Ancient Indian poets and intellectuals, via their compositions, honored the beauty, diversity, and spiritual richness of the region. They did this by praising the qualities of the area.

The literary sentiments that may be found in works such as "Shakuntala" by Kalidasa and the lyrics of classical poets depict vivid portraits of Bharatvarsha. The persistent imagery of "Bharat" as a realm of natural grandeur and cultural riches is contributed to by these literary compositions, which not only demonstrate the aesthetic sensitivities of the ancient inhabitants but also contribute to the preservation of this image.

Bharat, as described in the Upanishads, is the philosophical vision

The Upanishads, which are philosophical books that investigate the essence of reality and the self, also dive into the concept of "Bharat." The Upanishads, despite the fact that they do not use the term explicitly, communicate the profound insights and spiritual vision that have undoubtedly played a significant role in shaping the cultural landscape of the Indian subcontinent.

A comprehensive comprehension of existence, interdependence, and the quest for self-realization is what the Upanishads hope to convey to their readers. This philosophical perspective, which is frequently referred to as the everlasting philosophy of "Sanatana Dharma," serves as the foundation for the idea of "Bharat" as a repository of enduring wisdom and spiritual truths.

Trade and cultural exchanges dating back to ancient times: the context of Bharat in the world

There was not a period of isolation on the ancient Indian subcontinent; rather, it was involved in considerable cultural and commercial connections with other civilizations. Interactions with Central Asia, the Middle East, and Southeast Asia were made easier by the Silk Road and other marine routes. It was through these interactions that the name "Bharat" became known beyond the confines of its physical location.

Travelers from other countries, like the Chinese pilgrims Fa Xian and Xuanzang, referred to the place they visited as "Brahmadesh" or "Buddhist country," highlighting the cultural and spiritual aspects that are linked with the region. The concept of "Bharat" consequently became a component of the larger narrative of the linkages between cultures all over the world.

Interpretations of Colonialism: Bharat When It Was Under British Rule

The name "Bharat" was reinterpreted during the time period of British colonial control, which occurred throughout the colonial era. The notion of "Bharat" went through a process of rediscovery and reclaiming by Indian scholars and politicians throughout the time that the British administration continued to use the term "India" as the dominant designation for the subcontinent.

During the 19th and 20th centuries, intellectuals such as Bankim Chandra Chattopadhyay and Swami Vivekananda evoked the concept of "Bharat" as a symbol of cultural renaissance and national identity. This occurred as the nationalist movement gathered speed. During the fight for independence, the slogan "Bharat Mata" (Mother India) became a rallying cry. This phrase was used to refer to the nation as a personification.

Following the attainment of independence, Bharat and India engaged in constitutional discussions

An important turning point in the process of conceiving of the nation's name occurred during the period that followed the country's independence. Both "Bharat" and "India" were considered by the people who drafted the Constitution of India, but they ultimately decided to go with "India" as the official name of the nation.

The constitutional compromise led to the approval of both names, with Article 1 saying that "India, that is Bharat, shall be a Union of States." Both names were adopted.

The constitutional decision that was made shows the nuanced knowledge of the historical, cultural, and linguistic components that are involved with both names. The terms "Bharat" and "India" are used interchangeably in the official nomenclature, which acknowledges the nation's having two distinct identities.

Within the context of the Indian subcontinent, the term "Bharat" encompasses not only linguistic labels but also the historical, mythical, and cultural aspects of the region. "Bharat" emerges as a dynamic and varied notion that has formed the identity of the region. From the mythological rulers of the Mahabharata to the philosophical insights of the Upanishads, from the lyrical expressions of Kalidasa to the global exchanges of the Silk Road, many aspects of "Bharat" have contributed to the formation of the region's identity.

The word "Bharat" has a strong resonance in the modern period, not only because it is a historical and cultural marker, but also because it is a sign of continuity that connects the past with the present. It is a reflection of the complexity of a nation that cherishes its ancient heritage while also managing the difficulties and opportunities of the modern world that the terms "Bharat" and "India" coexist. An understanding of the continuing legacy of "Bharat" and the relevance of its role in the ongoing narrative of the Indian subcontinent can be gained through the investigation of these ancient roots.

2.1 Exploration of the ancient name "Bharat" and its significance

In the rich fabric of the Indian subcontinent's cultural, historical, and mythological traditions, the name "Bharat" holds a sacred position. One may trace its origins back to ancient literature, mythological narratives, and historical situations, where it appears not only as a linguistic label but also as a sign of identity, continuity, and cultural richness. Its roots can be traced back to these places. This investigation digs into the centuries-old name "Bharat," illuminating its roots, mythical underpinnings, historical connotations, and the continuing significance it has had in molding the collective psyche of the region.

In the Epics, Bharat is a character with mythological roots

There is a strong connection between the ancient term "Bharat" and Hindu mythology, specifically in the Mahabharata and the Ramayana, which are considered to be two of the most important Indian epics. According to the Mahabharata, Bharat is a legendary ruler whose family tree plays a significant part in determining the course of events that would occur on the Indian subcontinent.

His reign is frequently recognized as a time of prosperity, justice, and righteousness. He is the son of King Dushyanta and Queen Shakuntala, and his reign is a period of time that is celebrated.

It is via the Mahabharata that the genealogy of King Bharata is traced, hence laying the legendary groundwork for the name "Bharat." Through the weaving together of tales of bravery, virtue, and familial ties, the story transforms Bharat into a symbolic person that embodies the principles of dharma (righteousness) and responsible governance.

Bharat is the younger brother of Lord Rama, according to the text of the Ramayana. He exemplifies the principles of duty, loyalty, and sacrifice by his unshakable devotion to Rama and his refusal to rise to the throne in Rama's absence. The depiction of Bharat in these epics contributes to the legendary significance of the name, which, in addition to symbolizing historical characters, also represents archetypal symbols that symbolize virtuous government and familial duty.

Bharatvarsha and other ancient territories are associated with historical connotations

The name "Bharat" has become synonymous with the geographical breadth of the Indian subcontinent, transcending the world of mythology in the process. Ancient literature such as the Puranas make use of the term "Bharatvarsha" to refer to the territory that was controlled by King Bharata. As a result of this historical connotation, the term "Bharat" is transformed from a legendary name into a geographical identity that may be experienced.

Bharatvarsha is an area that is mentioned in the Puranas as being between the Himalayas in the north and the Indian Ocean in the south, spanning from the eastern seas to the western seas. The conception of "Bharat" as not simply a kingdom but rather a wide and diverse country with a shared cultural history was established as a result of this delineation, which set the foundation for the concept. The historical connotations that are associated with the term "Bharat" are therefore a contributing factor to the name's consistent relevance.

There is a unifying force in diversity that is cultural significance

In addition to its historical and mythological origins, the term "Bharat" carries with it a significant cultural significance over time. It acts as a unifying factor that brings together the various groups of the Indian subcontinent, which are diverse in terms of their languages, ethnicities, and religious beliefs. The word "Bharat" encapsulates the shared heritage, values, and traditions that have developed over the course of millennia throughout India.

The idea of "Bharat" as a cultural entity can be seen mirrored in historical works of art, literary works, and philosophical discourse. Bharatvarsha is envisioned as a sacred venue for the manifestation of arts and culture in the Natya Shastra, which is an ancient treatise on performing arts. A significant source of inspiration for the classical dance forms, music, and literature that have flourished in the region is the cultural ethos that is entrenched in the concept of "Bharat."

In the face of linguistic and regional variety, the term "Bharat" becomes a symbol that brings people together. By providing a collective umbrella that the numerous cultural manifestations of the subcontinent can find resonance within, it transcends the individuality of individual people.

Compositions of literature and poetic expressions created in the Sanskrit language

Sanskrit literature has been a vital component in the process of articulating the cultural and historical significance of the name "Bharat." This is due to the fact that it comprises a rich tapestry of poetry and prose, which makes it a crucial contribution to the process. By means of their compositions, ancient Indian poets and philosophers paid tribute to the region's aesthetic splendor, cultural diversity, and significant spiritual wealth. By praising the qualities of the location, they were able to accomplish this.

The poet Kalidasa, who is frequently considered to be among the most brilliant poets in Sanskrit literature, made a considerable contribution to the literary expressions that are associated with the state of "Bharat." His work, which is titled "Shakuntala," provides a vivid depiction of the natural splendor and cultural majesty that are present in the region. In their poems, classical poets paint vivid depictions of a vibrant and bustling "Bharat," thereby capturing the essence of the country's landscapes, festivals, and societal ideals to a significant degree.

Not only do these literary expressions illustrate the creative sensibilities of the ancients, but they also contribute to the everlasting concept of "Bharat" as a land that is endowed with both natural splendor and cultural treasures.

According to the Upanishads, Bharat is the philosophical perspective that guides human behavior

An enormous collection of ancient philosophical writings known as the Upanishads provides a profound perspective that is in agreement with the concept of "Bharat" as something that is more than merely a geographical entity. This perspective is offered by the Upanishads. However, despite the fact that the Upanishads do not make frequent use of the name "Bharat," they do communicate a holistic perspective on existence, interconnectedness, and the aspiration to achieve self-realization.

The notion of "Sanatana Dharma," which is commonly translated as the "perennial philosophy," draws its foundation from a philosophical perspective that can be found in the Upanishads. This perspective serves as the foundation for the concept.

This worldview, which is not limited by time or place, acknowledges the interconnection of all forms of life and has the ability to look beyond the transient. A better understanding of "Bharat" as a repository of knowledge that has endured the test of time and spiritual vision is made possible by the spiritual truths that are included within the Upanishads.

The backdrop of Bharat in the globe is characterized by the presence of trade and cultural exchanges that date back to ancient times

The ancient Indian subcontinent did not experience a time of isolation; rather, it was engaged in significant cultural and commercial contacts with other civilizations. This was the case throughout its history. Interactions with Southeast Asia, Central Asia, and the Middle East were simplified as a result of the Silk Road and other maritime routes. Because of these contacts, the name "Bharat" extended beyond the bounds of its physical location and became known to a wider audience.

Those who traveled from other countries, such as the Chinese pilgrims Fa Xian and Xuanzang, referred to the location they visited as "Brahmadesh" or "Buddhist country," so drawing attention to the cultural and spiritual qualities that are associated with the region. As a consequence of this, the idea of "Bharat" made its way into the larger narrative of the connections that exist between cultures all over the world.

Various interpretations of colonialism, including rediscovery and land reclamation

During the time period of British colonial control, which existed during the entire colonial era, the name "Bharat" was reinterpreted in a different way. As long as the British administration continued to use the term "India" as the predominant designation for the subcontinent, the concept of "Bharat" went through a process of rediscovery and reclaiming by Indian scholars and politicians. This process took place during the time that the British administration continued to use the term "India."

Intellectuals such as Bankim Chandra Chattopadhyay and Swami Vivekananda, who lived in the 19th and 20th centuries, were responsible for evoking the concept of "Bharat" as a symbol of cultural revival and national identity. This transpired at a time when the nationalist movement was gaining momentum. As a rallying cry during the struggle for independence, the phrase "Bharat Mata" (which translates to "Mother India") became popular. As a personification of the nation, this phrase was used to refer to the nation.

There was a reinvigorated appreciation for the historic term "Bharat" as a symbol of resistance against colonial rule during this time period. Additionally, there was a reaffirmation of cultural pride during this time period. As a result of the name's rise to popularity in literary and philosophical discussions, it eventually became an indispensable component of the narrative of Indian identity.

Following the attainment of independence, Bharat and India engaged in debates regarding the constitution

It was during the time period that followed the country's independence that a significant turning point happened in the process of conceiving of the name of the nation. Both "Bharat" and "India" were taken into consideration by the individuals who were responsible for drafting the Constitution of India; nevertheless, in the end, they reached the conclusion that "India" would be the most appropriate name for the nation. Article 1 of the Constitution states that "India, that is Bharat, shall be a Union of States." This Constitutional compromise resulted in the approval of both names. It was decided to use both names.

The conclusion that was taken about the constitutionality of both names demonstrates a deep understanding of the historical, cultural, and linguistic aspects that are associated with both names. In the official nomenclature, the terms "Bharat" and "India" are used interchangeably. This is done to acknowledge the fact that the nation possesses two separate identities.

Having an Understanding of the Significance of the Word "Bharat" in the Contemporary Context:

The ancient name "Bharat" carries with it a significance that extends beyond the historical and cultural implications that are typically connected with it. This significance is derived from the fact that it is applied to the current world. The nation's identity is firmly entrenched in its deeply embedded tradition, and it serves as a symbol that ties the past with the present with the purpose of establishing a connection between the two.

"Bharat" is a word that serves as a unifying force that transcends distinctions in language, regionality, and religion. It is a reflection of the cultural identity of the Indian subcontinent. The cultural identity of the Indian subcontinent is exemplified by this particular aspect. The providing of a common thread serves to bring together the numerous ways in which Indian culture is expressed, ranging from the diverse religious traditions to the traditional arts. This is accomplished through the provision of a common thread.

India is a nation that is well-known for the vast cultural diversity that it possesses, and the name "Bharat" acts as a symbol that strives to promote a sense of shared heritage and national pride in the country. At the same time that it acknowledges the intricacy of cultural expressions that have emerged over the period of millennia, it supports the concept of unity in variety.

The use of the word "Bharat" signifies a dedication to the preservation of cultural heritage as well as the continuation of historical events. This dedication is demonstrated by the use of the word. It shows reverence for the ancient roots that are embedded in the Upanishads, the Mahabharata, and the Ramayana, as well as the philosophical wisdom that is included within these three epics. By utilizing the name "Bharat," India has established itself as a protector of a legacy that has persisted for a very long time and dates back to ancient times. This legacy has been passed down from generation to generation.

Through the growth of this sense of historical continuity, the relationships between the past, the present, and the future are brought into closer proximity with one another. It encourages the development of a communal consciousness that acknowledges the significance of the ancients' contributions to culture, spirituality, and philosophy and then tries to preserve those contributions wherever it is feasible to do so.

Philosophical and spiritual components and factors The intellectual foundations that are linked with the name "Bharat" resonate with the spiritual components that are ingrained in Indian philosophy. These elements are important to the Indian philosophical tradition. An individual who is committed to the exploration of higher ideals, the cultivation of their own potential, and the recognition of the interdependence of all forms of life is said to have this trait. At a time when the world is struggling to come to terms with the challenges of modern existence, the name "Bharat" serves as a reminder of these essentially timeless philosophical values.

"Bharat" is not merely a geographical name; rather, it symbolizes a holistic vision that combines factors such as ethical values, spiritual awareness, and a harmonious coexistence with the natural world. This is because "Bharat" is not restricted to a basic geographical designation. It is in accordance with the broad goals of sustainable development and the well-being of the entire globe that this all-encompassing approach is implemented.

In this post-colonial era, the name "Bharat" has come to be interchangeable with both the concept of national pride and the concept of cultural revival. Therefore, this is due to the fact that the term "Bharat" incorporates both of these ideas. All of these things are symbolized by this: a reaffirmation of cultural autonomy, a rejection of colonial impositions, and a reclaiming of one's identity. The invocation of "Bharat Mata" at the time of the independence movement perfectly encapsulated the spirit of cultural pride and resiliency that was present at the time.

The use of the term "Bharat" in the contemporary context suggests that an individual is making a concerted effort to distinguish themselves from the legacies of colonialism and to develop an identity that is both independent and culturally rooted.

Not only does it serve as a declaration of self-assertion, but it also serves as a celebration of the wealthy cultural tapestry that the nation possesses.

In spite of the fact that the name "Bharat" is considered to have important cultural and historical value inside the subcontinent, it is also known on a worldwide scale, which is advantageous for diplomatic purposes. The use of the term "Bharat" in international diplomacy and other types of global interaction reveals a connection to long-standing customs as well as a distinct identity at the same time.

The term "Bharat" is a significant contributor to a unique worldwide identity that is not merely a geographical location but rather a civilization that has a long and illustrious history. The process of India's engagement with the international community is resulting in the development of this identity. At the same time as it draws attention to India as a repository of ancient knowledge and contemporary vitality, it also adds a layer of cultural depth to India's involvement on the international stage.

In the course of the inquiry into the ancient word "Bharat," a complex tapestry that is woven together with threads of mythology, history, culture, and philosophy has been revealed. Not only does its relevance extend beyond the boundaries of language categories, but it also incorporates a cultural identity that has survived for millennia. From the mythological rulers of the Mahabharata to the philosophical insights of the Upanishads, from the visual manifestations of ancient arts to the challenges of colonial reinterpretations, "Bharat" emerges as a phrase that is both dynamic and ageless. It is a name that encompasses all of these aspects of Indian culture.

The use of the name "Bharat" in relation to the present day is indicative of a purposeful decision to embrace historical continuity, cultural richness, and a distinct identity pertaining to the present day. In addition to fostering a sense of national pride and making a contribution to a global recognition that is not limited by geographical limits, it also serves as a unifying force that works to bring people together.

As India advances forward into the future, the name "Bharat" serves as a guiding light for the country. The capacity to firmly entrenched the nation in its historical legacy while also managing the challenges of the modern world is a capability that it possesses. The research of this ancient phrase has the potential to lead to a more thorough understanding of the cultural inheritance that continues to play a vital role in the construction of the identity of the Indian subcontinent.

2.2 Historical and cultural references to Bharat in ancient texts

A profound resonance may be found within the historical and cultural fabric of the Indian subcontinent when the name "Bharat" is considered. This phrase, which has its origins in ancient literature, represents a rich tapestry of mythology, history, and cultural identity. It transcends language classifications and is rooted in ancient manuscripts. The purpose of this investigation is to investigate the historical and cultural references to the term "Bharat" that can be found in ancient manuscripts. By doing so, the significance and multidimensional nature of this respected name will be revealed.

Bharat, as shown in the Mahabharata, from the Buddhist perspective

The Mahabharata, which is considered to be one of the longest epic poems in the world, is the primary work that serves as the basis for the name "Bharat." One of the most important figures in its lines is the legendary monarch Bharata, who bestows his name onto the territory that would later be known as Bharatvarsha after it was established.

An account of the family tree of King Bharata, who was the son of King Dushyanta and Queen Shakuntala, is included in the Mahabharata. The reign of Bharata is portrayed as a time of prosperity and righteousness, with an emphasis on the principles of dharma (righteous duty) and good governance from the perspective of the story. One of the factors that contributes to the legendary significance of "Bharat" as a figure of righteous leadership is his status as a paragon of virtue and responsible rulership.

Not only does the Mahabharata, with its intricate tale, present King Bharata as a historical figure, but it also firmly establishes the name inside the cultural consciousness of the cultural community that resides on the Indian subcontinent. An identification of the word "Bharat" with the territory that covers modern-day India is established through the epic, which provides the framework for this association.

The Bharat as a Symbol of Devotion and Duty in the Tale of the Ramayana

Within the Ramayana, which is another beloved epic of Indian literature, Bharat plays a part that is distinct from the others but is nonetheless of similar importance. It is through Bharat, the younger brother of Lord Rama, that the concept of unshakable loyalty and selfless duty is brought to life.

During the time that Lord Rama is banished from Ayodhya, Bharat, despite being granted the throne, stubbornly refuses to assume the position of king in his absence. Rather than that, he sits on the throne and administers the kingdom on Rama's behalf by placing his sandals on the seat. Cultural qualities that have stood the test of time include Bharat's unwavering devotion to his older brother and his unwavering loyalty to dharma.

Through the character of Bharat, the Ramayana serves to reinforce the cultural ethos that is associated with the origin of the term. The term "Bharat" is more than just a historical name; it is also a symbol of the relationships that exist among families, loyalty, and the commitment to ethical standards.

The Bharatvarsha Puranas and the Concept of Geographical Identity

The Puranas, which are a type of ancient Indian literature, are a significant contributor to the establishment of the geographical identity of "Bharat" by the use of the term "Bharatvarsha." The huge territory that extends from the Himalayas in the north to the Indian Ocean in the south, as well as from the eastern seas to the western seas, is referred to by this designation.

In ancient books such as the Vishnu Purana and the Bhagavata Purana, the region known as Bharatvarsha is portrayed as a sacred place that is characterized by its numerous ecosystems, mighty rivers, and revered pilgrimage destinations. Not only do the Puranas give the word a cultural and religious importance, but they also express the geographical borders of the region.

The notion of Bharatvarsha, which is found in the Puranas, serves as a uniting identifier for the region. It highlights the shared cultural legacy and spiritual value that connects the many landscapes of the subcontinent together.

Literature written in Sanskrit: poetic expressions of the beauty of Rajasthan

The literary works written in Sanskrit, which are distinguished by their poetic depth, have made a substantial contribution to the cultural references that are connected with the term "Bharat." By employing vivid descriptions in works such as "Shakuntala" and "Meghaduta," poets such as Kalidasa are able to illustrate the natural beauty and cultural riches of Bharatvarsha.

The lyrics of Kalidasa conjure up images of imposing mountains, gushing rivers, and abundant flora and wildlife, thus conveying the spirit of a region that is not just topographical but also a source of aesthetic inspiration. The cultural perception of Bharat as a land of unsurpassed beauty and cultural richness is influenced by these lyrical expressions, which contribute to the perception.

For the purpose of enhancing the cultural identity that is linked with the word "Bharat," the literary compositions of Kalidasa and other classical poets serve to create a literary heritage that continues to inspire artistic expressions in the region.

Natya Shastra: The Importance of Bharatvarsha in Ancient Indian Culture

The concept of Bharatvarsha is incorporated into the cultural discourse of the Natya Shastra, which is an ancient treatise on performing arts that is attributed to the wise Bharata Muni. With the intention of serving as a sacred venue for the expression of arts and culture, Bharatvarsha is envisioned.

Although the Natya Shastra acknowledges the various cultural traditions that exist throughout Bharatvarsha, it places a strong emphasis on the significance of blending regional variances and a wide range of art forms into the practice of performing arts. This recognition of the cultural diversity that exists within the geographical expanse of Bharat imparts an additional degree of significance to the cultural relevance of the region.

The treatise written by Bharata Muni not only positions the practice of performing arts within the larger context of cultural identity and legacy, but it also sets principles for the performing arts itself.

Philosophical Insights and the Spiritual Significance of Bharat are Presented in the Upanishads

Through the transmission of profound insights into spirituality and the nature of existence, the Upanishads, which are recognized as the philosophical texts of ancient

India, contribute to the cultural references of Bharat. The teachings of the Upanishads are consistent with the spiritual aspects that are connected with the name "Bharat," despite the fact that the Upanishads do not use the term "Bharat" directly.

An investigation into the nature of the self, the interdependence of all existence, and the quest for self-realization are all topics that are covered in the Upanishads. These philosophical truths, which are frequently referred to as the "perennial philosophy" or "Sanatana Dharma," constitute the spiritual foundation that serves as the basis for the cultural identity of Bharat.

To the cultural references that are associated with Bharat, the Upanishads provide a philosophical dimension by means of their examination of timeless truths. This highlights the role that Bharat plays as a repository of spiritual learning.

International Cultural Exchanges: India's Position in International Accounts

There was not a period of isolation on the ancient Indian subcontinent; rather, it was involved in considerable cultural and commercial connections with other civilizations.

In records that were written by foreign visitors and historians, such as Fa Xian and Xuanzang from China, the region was referred to as "Brahmadesh" or the "Buddhist country." These individuals chronicled their experiences traveling through the region.

As seen from the outside, these testimonies from other countries offer a look into the cultural and religious variety that exists within the country of Bharat. As a result of the exchange of ideas, artistic creations, and philosophical perspectives that took place during these interactions, the cultural references that are linked with the name "Bharat" on a global scale were further enriched.

Rediscovery and different interpretations of the Colonial Era

The period of time known as the colonial era was a period of significant change in the history of Bharat, as it was during this time that the country was ruled by the British. As Indian intellectuals and politicians attempted to regain their cultural identity, the concept of "Bharat" witnessed a comeback. This occurred despite the fact that the British administration used the term "India" in official papers the majority of the time.

During the fight for independence, intellectuals such as Bankim Chandra Chattopadhyay and Swami Vivekananda called attention to the concept of "Bharat" as a symbol of cultural revitalization and national pride. The word evolved into a rallying cry against the impositions of colonial rule and a call for the rebirth of indigenous customs and practices respectively.

Bharat's significance as a symbol of cultural autonomy and resistance was strengthened as a result of this moment of rediscovery, which helped to a revived awareness of the historical and cultural references linked with Bharat.

A colorful portrayal of a term that goes beyond basic geographical or political designations is painted by the historical and cultural references to "Bharat" that may be found in ancient literature. From the mythological stories told in the Mahabharata to the poetic expressions found in Sanskrit literature, from the philosophical insights found in the Upanishads to the cultural significance found in the Natya Shastra, the term "Bharat" emerges as a multifaceted concept that is deeply intertwined with the identity of the Indian subcontinent.

"Bharat" is not a static name; rather, it is a dynamic term that has evolved over the course of millennia with each new layer of cultural, intellectual, and historical significance introduced.

In the Mahabharata, "Bharat" is a sign of righteous government; in the Ramayana, it is a symbol of unshakable devotion; in Sanskrit literature, it is a symbol of cultural richness; and in the Upanishads, it is a symbol of spiritual insight. All of these symbols capture the vast cultural history that has influenced the region.

The investigation of these references not only contributes to a deeper comprehension of the history, but it also elucidates the everlasting significance of the term "Bharat" in the context of the present day. As India moves forward into the future, the word "Bharat" acts as a cultural anchor, connecting the present with its ancient roots and promoting a sense of continuity and pride in the rich heritage of the Indian subcontinent. This was accomplished by connecting the present with its roots.

2.3 Examining linguistic and cultural diversity across the subcontinent

The Indian subcontinent is a patchwork of linguistic and cultural diversity, unparalleled in its depth and breadth of the linguistic and cultural diversity it possesses. From the snow-capped peaks of the Himalayas to the tropical coastlines of the Indian Ocean, this huge territory is home to a rich tapestry of languages, faiths, traditions, and customs. It stretches from the Himalayas to the Indian Ocean. A closer look at the linguistic and cultural diversity that exists across the subcontinent sheds light on the complex interplay of history, geography, and social forces that have contributed to the formation of the identities of the various populations that make up the subcontinent.

A Towering Tapestry in the Form of Linguistic Diversity

India possesses a linguistic diversity that is unmatched anywhere else in the world, making it a veritable kaleidoscope of languages. The People's Linguistic Survey of India counts more than 780 languages, which is a reflection of the great linguistic plurality that exists in India. The Constitution of India acknowledges 22 languages that are officially acknowledged.

Languages of the Indo-Aryan Family: The majority of the total population of India is able to communicate in languages that are members of the Indo-Aryan family. As the language that is spoken the most and acts as the lingua franca of the nation, Hindi is the language that is spoken the most by the most people. Bengali, Punjabi, Marathi, Gujarati, and Oriya are some of the other important Indo-Aryan languages among those spoken today.

Languages of the Dravidian family: South India is distinguished by the prevalence of languages belonging to the Dravidian family. Malayalam, Tamil, Telugu, and Kannada are the four most important Dravidian languages.

Each of these languages has its own distinctive script and cultural peculiarities. When it comes to the cultural history of the region, Tamil, with its long-standing literary tradition, has a unique and significant role.

Sino-Tibetan Languages: The majority of the languages spoken in the states located in the northeastern region are members of the Sino-Tibetan language family. Some examples of languages that are spoken in this region include Assamese, Bodo, and Manipuri. Each of these languages contributes to the linguistic mosaic that forms the subcontinent.

Languages such as Santali, which are spoken by the Adivasi groups, are examples of languages that belong to the Austroasiatic family. Other language families include Sanskrit and other languages. In addition, varieties of languages belonging to the Austroasiatic and Andamanese families, such as Mundari and Great Andamanese, are a significant contributor to the linguistic diversity that exists in particular places.

The linguistic variety of India is not limited to main language families; rather, it encompasses a large number of dialects, variants, and scripts. This results in a linguistic landscape that is reflective of the historical, cultural, and geographical complexities of the subcontinent.

Religious diversity: The Indian subcontinent is a cradle of major world faiths, including Hinduism, Buddhism, Jainism, and Sikhism, as well as subsequent influences of Islam and Christianity. Cultural diversity emphasizes the importance of celebrating pluralism. Each religion brings with it its own distinctive set of customs, rituals, and celebrations, which all contribute to the rich tapestry of religious diversity.

There are a great number of deities, rituals, and intellectual schools that are practised within Hinduism, which is the largest religion. Both Jainism and Buddhism, which both have their roots in ancient India, have left an unmistakable influence on the cultural and architectural history of the region. The development of Sikhism throughout the medieval period adds yet another dimension to the religious variety that exists.

Islamic culture emerged as a significant cultural and religious influence once it was brought to the region through trade and conquest. There is a huge and diversified Muslim community in India, and there are geographical differences in the rituals and traditions that are observed by Muslims. Europe's colonial powers were responsible for the introduction of Christianity, which has since found a place among a variety of communities.

Festivals and Traditions: The subcontinent is home to a plethora of festivals, each of which is associated with a particular religious or cultural tradition. Some examples of holidays that are celebrated with fervor in a variety of societies are Diwali, Holi, Eid, Christmas, Navratri, and Baisakhi. These are just a few instances. The feeling of communal harmony is often fostered because of the fact that these festivities frequently cross religious borders.

As diverse as the languages spoken on the subcontinent, the culinary scene of the subcontinent is also rather varied. It is true that every location has its own distinctive flavors, spices, and methods of preparation. Indian cuisine is a gastronomic experience that reflects the diversity of civilizations. From the rich and aromatic biryanis of the north to the spicy curries of the south, from the sweets of Bengal to the street food pleasures of Mumbai, Indian cuisine is a gourmet trip.

Art and Architecture: The art and architecture of the subcontinent are different from one location to another because they are influenced by different historical periods, different rulers, and different social relations. There are many things that contribute to the rich cultural history of India, including the detailed carvings of temples in Khajuraho, the Mughal architecture of the Taj Mahal, the bright frescoes of Rajasthan, and the Dravidian architecture of temples in South India.

Dress and Attire: The traditional dress used in different locations shows a great deal of variation. The vivid sarees of Gujarat, the elaborate silk sarees of Kanchipuram, the phulkari of Punjab, and the traditional dress of a variety of tribal populations are all examples of the different sartorial expressions that are present.

Dynasties and empires have had a significant impact on the cultural landscape

A series of dynasties and empires have played a significant role in shaping the historical trajectory of the subcontinent. Each of these dynasties and empires has left its mark on the cultural landscape. A number of historical figures, including the Mauryas, Guptas, Cholas, and Mughals, as well as the British Empire, have been instrumental in the formation of the many identities of the people who currently reside in this region.

The Mughal Empire: The Mughals, who ruled over huge portions of the Indian subcontinent from the 16th to the 19th century, had a significant role in the development of cultural fusion. There are two permanent legacies that have been left behind by this time period: the Mughal architecture, which includes buildings such as the Taj Mahal, and the establishment of the Urdu language.

The Vijayanagara Empire: The Vijayanagara Empire left an everlasting mark on the art and architecture of the southern region. The architectural prowess of this medieval empire is on full display in the city of Hampi, which is home to a number of magnificent temples and ruins.

The time of British Colonialism: Although the time of British colonial rule was characterized by exploitation and subjection, it also brought about cultural contacts and transformations. Since its introduction throughout this time period, the English language has developed into a prominent component of the linguistic landscape, particularly in the fields of administration and education specifically.

Regional Identities and Autonomy: Maintaining Individuality and Characteristics

The subcontinent is characterized by various regional identities that have managed to preserve their individuality over the course of millennia, despite the overall diversity that exists around it. A number of states, like Kerala, Punjab, Bengal, Tamil Nadu, and Gujarat, each have their own unique languages, cultural customs, and traditions, all of which contribute to the overall diversity of the federal government.

South India: South India, which has its roots in Dravidian culture and language, possesses a cultural identity that is both distinct and distinctively its own. Classical dance styles such as Bharatanatyam, Carnatic music, and the architectural style of the Dravidians are all distinguishing characteristics of the cultural landscape in this region.

North India: North India is distinguished by its Indo-Aryan language influences, which are exemplified by the presence of classical dance styles such as Kathak, Hindustani classical music, and architectural marvels such as the Qutub Minar and Red Fort in Delhi.

Northern States: The northern states, where there are a variety of ethnic groups and languages, have their own distinct cultural identities. Several states, like Manipur, Assam, and Nagaland, have rich cultural traditions that contribute to the complex tapestry of cultural variety. These traditions include traditional attire, festivals, and folk traditions.

Western India: The two states of Maharashtra, Gujarat, and Rajasthan, which are located in western India, each have their own distinct manifestations of culture. The cultural identity of this region is mostly composed of elements such as the Marathi language, the lively festivals of Gujarat, and the folk traditions of Rajasthan.

Bengal, which is located in eastern India, is home to a thriving literary and cultural legacy throughout the country. The cultural landscape of this region is characterized by a number of distinguishing characteristics, including the Bengali language, Rabindra Sangeet, and the lively festivals of Durga Puja.

Change Management in the Context of Globalization's Impact

There is no way to avoid the effects of globalization in the 21st century, and the Indian subcontinent is not an exception. There has been a mingling of cultures and the emergence of a cosmopolitan mindset as a result of increased connectedness, migration, and technological breakthroughs. Despite the fact that globalization has resulted in cultural exchanges and impacts, it also presents obstacles to the preservation of traditional customs and languages.

Urbanization: Because of the global nature of urban areas, they frequently serve as a melting pot for people from a variety of cultural backgrounds. People from a variety of linguistic and cultural origins live in metropolitan areas such as Mumbai, Delhi, and Bangalore, which results in a fusion of traditions. These cities become melting pots.

Media and Technology: The proliferation of digital media and technology has made it easier for people all over the world to communicate their thoughts and views and to express their cultural identities. The internet, social media platforms, and streaming platforms have all evolved into platforms that facilitate the distribution of varied cultural content, which in turn has an effect on how individuals view and interact with their own diverse cultures.

Language Dynamics: English, which is a lingua franca recognized all over the world, has become increasingly prevalent in metropolitan areas and corporate contexts. Despite the fact that it is a medium of communication, particularly in the context of globalization, it also presents obstacles to the preservation of indigenous languages.

Homogenization of Culture and Resistance: The global flow of information and cultural products has given rise to concerns regarding the homogenization of cultures. There is, however, a significant opposition to such standardization, with communities actively seeking to maintain and promote their distinctive cultural practices. This resistance is taking place among communities.

An investigation of the linguistic and cultural diversity that exists across the Indian subcontinent reveals a complex tapestry that is woven with the threads of history, geography, and the dynamics of social behavior.

The diversity of the subcontinent is not simply the juxtaposition of different elements; rather, it is the result of a dynamic interplay of cultures that have developed over the course of millennia.

As the subcontinent navigates the currents of globalization, the problem comes in striking a balance between embracing the benefits that come with interconnectedness and conserving the distinctive identities that distinguish each linguistic and cultural community. This is a challenge that the subcontinent faces. Providing a foundation for creating unity in diversity is a defining trait that continues to influence the cultural landscape of the Indian subcontinent. This foundation is provided by the resiliency of the many communities that are spread over the subcontinent, as well as an appreciation for the legacy that they share.

Chapter 3

The Vedic Era and Beyond

As a significant era in the annals of Indian history, the Vedic era serves as the basis upon which the various cultural, religious, and philosophical traditions of the subcontinent have thrived. This era is known as the Vedic period. This period, which has its origins in the sacred scriptures known as the Vedas, encompasses a significant amount of time and historical period, during which it witnessed the development of society institutions, religious rituals, and philosophical discourses. During the time period that follows the Vedic period, India's historical landscape undergoes a series of dynamic upheavals. These transitions are characterized by the rise and fall of empires, the incorporation of other cultures, and the development of deep philosophical systems. Within the scope of this investigation, we delve into the myriad of facets that comprise the Vedic age and trace the trajectories of Indian culture beyond how it developed during this time period.

A General Introduction to the Vedic Period

Chronology and the Situation:

After the Vedas, which are a collection of religious hymns and ceremonies penned in Sanskrit, the Vedic age, which is commonly dated from approximately 1500 BCE to 500 BCE, is named after the compilation. The Rigvedic period and the later Vedic period are the two primary stages that are traditionally considered to be the two main phases of this period. The former is connected to the Rigveda, which is the earliest of the Vedas, while the latter is the witness to the composition of the Samaveda, Yajurveda, and Atharvaveda.

The Sarasvati River is believed to be a key part of the geographical environment that existed during the Vedic period, which encompasses the northern area of the Indian subcontinent. The Vedic people, who are frequently referred to as Aryans, are thought to have migrated into the Indian subcontinent around this time period, which coincides with the demise of the civilization that flourished in the Indus Valley.

As for the economy and society:

There are four different varnas that are described in the Rigveda. These varnas are as follows: Brahmins, who are considered to be priests and scholars; Kshatriyas, who are considered to be warriors and rulers; Vaishyas, who are considered to be farmers and merchants; and Shudras, who are considered to be laborers and service providers.

The caste system, which would later become pervasive across Indian civilization, was established on the foundation of this varna system.

The Vedic people were mostly involved in agriculture and pastoralism as their predominant economic activities. In their civilization, the cow was considered to be a sign of riches and success, and it had a central position. The Vedic scriptures provide evidence of the transition from a nomadic way of life to agricultural societies that were settled down.

Philosophy and Religious Thinking:

The pantheon of deities plays a significant role in the religious landscape of the Vedic age. Indra, Agni, Varuna, and Mitra are among the deities that have major places in this pantheon. Vedic religious traditions included the recitation of Vedic hymns in addition to the performance of rites that involved the offering of sacrifices. These ceremonies were referred to as yajnas.

In terms of philosophy, the hymns of the Rigveda are where the ideas that form the foundation of Indian philosophical thought are expressed. The idea of rita, which refers to the order and truth of the cosmos, served as the basis for subsequent developments in philosophical inquiry. Exploring the nature of reality and the self, the later Vedic literature, particularly the Upanishads, dive into profound metaphysical and speculative notions. These texts are particularly notable for their content.

Transitions Following the Vedic Period

The period of the Epic and Puranic era:

The transition from the Vedic period to the Epic and Puranic periods results in a change in the way that religious and literary expressions are expressed. There is a narrative framework that is provided by the two great epics, the Mahabharata and the Ramayana. This framework encompasses moral and ethical difficulties, heroic deeds, and heavenly interventions. In addition, the Puranas, which are a type of ancient Indian literature, provide tales of mythology and cosmology, and they also serve as a repository of religious knowledge.

Empires of the Maurya and Gupta types:

As a result of the establishment of powerful empires, the political landscape of ancient India went through tremendous upheavals. Chandragupta Maurya and his successors were responsible for the unification of a significant portion of the Indian subcontinent under the Maurya Empire, which lasted from 322 BCE to 185 BCE. Buddhism was spread throughout India by Emperor Ashoka, who was also a proponent of nonviolent values. He was a significant character in Indian history.

For many people, the Gupta Empire, which lasted from about 320 to 550 CE, is considered to be the "Golden Age" of ancient Indian civilization. Chandragupta I, Samudragupta, and Chandragupta II were some of the Gupta kings that were responsible for the flourishing of the arts, sciences, and literature throughout their reign. The idea of zero and the decimal system were both introduced into Indian mathematics during this time period. Additionally, the classical Sanskrit literary tradition reached its pinnacle during this time period.

The propagation of Jainism and Buddhism:

The period after the Vedic period was marked by the rise of new religious movements that posed a challenge to the traditional Brahmanical practices. Buddhism was established in the sixth century BCE by Siddhartha Gautama, who would later be known as Buddha. He was the one who first articulated the Four Noble Truths and the Eightfold Path. around India and beyond, Buddhism gained tremendous support and expanded around the world.

The Jain religion, which was founded by Mahavira and was contemporaneous with Buddhism, placed an emphasis on nonviolence, truth, and austere disciplines. In addition to challenging the hierarchical framework of Vedic society, Buddhism and Jainism both advocated for alternate ways to achieve spiritual enlightenment among their followers.

The Classical Era, Beginning with the Gupta and Ending with the Medieval Period

The fall of the Gupta dynasty and the regions' kingdoms:

The Gupta Empire eventually fell into disrepair as a result of internal warfare and external invasions, which ultimately led to the spread of political authority throughout the empire. There was a proliferation of regional kingdoms, each of which asserted its control over particular territory. The classical period was characterized by the on-going growth of art, literature, and philosophy, as well as the flourishing of traditional cultures from many regions.

Chola and Pallava Dynasties, respectively:

In the region of Southern India, the Chola and Pallava dynasties were instrumental in the formation of the political and cultural landscape. The Cholas, who were famous for their maritime trade and naval skill, established a flourishing civilization that had a significant and long-lasting influence on the art and architecture of the region. In addition to being patrons of the arts and literature, the Pallavas were also contributors to the development of Dravidian culture.

Within the context of the Delhi Sultanate, Islamic Invasions:

During the medieval period, Islamic empires arrived in India through invasions led by Mahmud of Ghazni and Muhammad Ghori. These assaults took place while India was still under Muslim rule. The establishment of the Delhi Sultanate in the thirteenth century was a significant event that signaled the consolidation of Muslim rule in northern India. The emergence of a syncretic Indo-Islamic culture during this time period established the foundation for the Mughal Empire that flourished in the years that followed.

Mughal Empire and the Arrival of Europeans in the Fourth Century

The Mughal Dynasty:

There is a key era in Indian history that is represented by the Mughal Empire, which was established by Babur in the year 1526. The empire reached its pinnacle under the reign of Akbar the Great, which was also the time when a cultural renaissance took place, which was characterized by religious tolerance, architectural marvels, and the blossoming of the arts. As an enduring representation of this time period, the Taj Mahal, which is a testimony to Mughal architecture, stands as a symbol.

The Exploration and Colonization Conducted by Europeans:

During the 15th and 16th centuries, European nations such as the Portuguese, Dutch, French, and English competed with one another for the position of dominant nation in commerce with India. After receiving a charter from the British crown, the East India Company progressively secured control over the areas that were located in India. The process of colonization in India had significant implications on the socioeconomic and cultural aspects of the country. These repercussions included the introduction of new technology, administrative structures, and religious influences.

As well as the Sikh Empire and the Maratha Confederacy:

The Maratha Confederacy arose as a powerful power in western India around the time that the Mughal empire was falling apart. Both territorial expansion and political intrigue were activities that the Marathas participated in, with charismatic leaders such as Chhatrapati Shivaji and, subsequently, Peshwas serving as their leaders. It was about the same time that Maharaja Ranjit Singh formed the Sikh Empire, which was responsible for establishing Sikh sovereignty in the northwestern portions of the subcontinent.

The British Raj and the Path to Independence

The East India Company and the Rule of the British:

Over time, the East India Company's commercial interests increasingly morphed into political authority, culminating in the formal formation of the British Raj in the year 1858. The control of the British had far-reaching effects on Indian society, including the introduction of modern education, railways, and administrative systems. However, the British also exploited resources and implemented policies that fanned discontent, which contributed to the situation.

Indian Independence Movement

There was a fierce nationalist movement that emerged during the 20th century. It was led by influential individuals such as Mahatma Gandhi, Jawaharlal Nehru, and Subhas Chandra Bose. Protests using nonviolent methods, acts of civil disobedience, and mass movements all played a significant role in convincing the British government to grant India its independence in 1947. India was divided into two nations, India and Pakistan, which marked the beginning of a turbulent chapter that was characterized by large-scale migrations and conflict between different communities.

India after it gained its independence:

In 1950, with its attainment of independence, India became a secular republic by adopting a democratic constitution. During the period following independence, nation-building, economic development, and social fairness were all concerns that were brought to the forefront. The political landscape of India has been marked by periods of coalition governments, economic reforms, and social transformations that have alternated with one another.

Diversity and Sustaining of Cultural Traditions

The arts and architecture:

India has a long and illustrious history of art and architecture, which contributes to the country's unique cultural fabric. Indian art is a reflection of the diverse cultural influences that have shaped the country, from the prehistoric cave temples of Ajanta and Ellora to the detailed carvings of Khajuraho and the architectural marvels of the Mughal era. Forts, palaces, mosques, and temples are all examples of buildings that serve as testaments to the artistic achievements of various time eras.

Philosophy and Comparative Literature:

The literary foundation of Indian culture is Sanskrit literature, which includes the Vedas, epics, and Upanishads, as well as classical works such as Kalidasa's "Shakuntala" and Bhasa's plays. Post-independence literature written in a variety of languages has made a significant contribution to the development of a sophisticated understanding of modern India. Intellectual inquiry and spiritual discovery are two things that continue to be inspired by Indian philosophy, regardless of whether it is founded in the Vedas, Upanishads, or subsequent works.

The celebrations and customs

The numerous celebrations and customs that India observes are a dynamic expression of the country's vibrant cultural diversity. A number of festivals, including Diwali, Holi, Eid, Durga Puja, and Navaratri, are celebrated with fervor, which reflects the nation's commitment to a heterogeneous culture. The transmission of traditional art forms, dance, music, and rituals from one generation to the next exemplifies the continuity of cultural activities.

The Vedic period, which is characterized by its philosophical inquiries, ritualistic activities, and social systems, is considered to be the foundation of India's significant cultural history. Future historical epochs, which were characterized by empires, invasions, and colonial rule, have played a significant role in shaping the outlines of modern India. In spite of these changes, India's cultural, religious, and philosophical traditions have managed to endure, which is a testament to the country's remarkable capacity for maintaining its civilizational continuity.

The path that has been traveled has been one of development and adaptation, beginning with the Vedic hymns that pondered the order of the universe and ending with the rich tapestry that is contemporary India. The enduring spirit of India can be characterized by the combination of a wide range of influences, the coexistence of a great number of traditions, and the never-ending pursuit of knowledge and spirituality. As the subcontinent works its way through the problems of the 21st century, its historical past continues to reverberate, offering insights into the complex relationship between tradition and transformation.

3.1 Discussion on the Vedic period and its impact on the region's nomenclature

The Vedic period, which was an important era in the history of the Indian sub-continent, has left an indelible impact on the nomenclature of the region. This period, which generally spans from 1500 BCE to 500 BCE, is distinguished by the compilation of the sacred scriptures known as the Vedas. These texts played a key role in shaping not only the religious and philosophical philosophy of the time, but also the cultural and physical landscape of the time. In this topic, we go into the Vedic period and investigate the enormous impact that it had on the nomenclature of the Indian subcontinent. We investigate the ways in which linguistic, cultural, and geographical aspects came together to produce a rich tapestry of names and designations.

The Vedic Period's Contributions to the Language of the World:

Sanskrit and the Vedas:

Sanskrit, an ancient Indo-Aryan language, was developed and refined throughout the Vedic period, which is considered to be the most important part of this period. This particular language was used to construct the Vedas, which are considered to be the most ancient sacred scriptures in the Hindu religion. These Vedas served as the basis for later literary and linguistic endeavors. The Rigveda, in example, is full of hymns that not only convey religious sentiments but also demonstrate the linguistic expertise of the people who lived throughout the Vedic period.

The development of Sanskrit languages during this time period had a significant and long-lasting effect on the nomenclature of the region. The language evolved into a medium through which religious, philosophical, and cultural concepts were communicated, in turn having an impact on the names of geographical features, rivers, and deities. The persistent linguistic heritage of the Vedic period is demonstrated by the fact that many contemporary Indian languages, such as Hindi, Bengali, and Marathi, can trace their roots back to Sanskrit.

The Geographic Significance of Place Names and Their Names:

The Vedic books offer a plethora of information regarding the geographical characteristics of the area, and many of the place names that are listed in the Vedas are still relevant in modern times. Rivers, mountains, and plains are frequently known by their names in hymns and rites, which demonstrates the profound connection that the Vedic people had with their natural environment.

An example of this would be the revered Sarasvati River, which is mentioned quite frequently in the Rigveda. This river occupies an important place in Vedic literature. There is a controversy among academics regarding whether or not the Sarasvati actually exists in the physical world; yet, the fact that it is mentioned in Vedic texts demonstrates the significance of rivers in the Vedic worldview. A number of rivers, including the Ganges, Yamuna, and others, are held in high esteem in Vedic literature, and the names of these rivers continue to reverberate in the geography of the region.

Nomenclature of the Cultural and Religious Traditions:

Deities and Concepts of the Cosmic Aspects:

The Vedic pantheon is filled with a large number of gods, each of whom is connected to a distinct set of characteristics, functions, and ideas about the cosmos.

Indra, Agni, Varuna, and Mitra are just some of the names that are intricately woven into the fabric of Vedic hymns. These names represent the cosmic forces and natural components. The significance of these deities extends beyond the realm of religion, and it has an impact on the naming practices that are used for particular locations and regions.

For instance, the term "Indraprastha" is found in ancient books, such as the Mahabharata, and it refers to a city that is thought to have been established by the Pandavas. This habit of identifying physical areas with divine entities is exemplified by the name, which is derived from the god Indra. The nomenclature in question not only demonstrates a reverence for the religious tradition, but it also makes a contribution to the cultural character of the region.

Worship and the Performance of Sacrifices:

Yajnas, which are elaborate rites of sacrifice, played a significant role in the religious and social lives of the Vedic people. These rituals are what distinguish the Vedic period from other periods. While these rituals are being performed, the hymns that are being chanted frequently contain names and epithets that emphasize the significance of particular deities and elements of the rite.

The nomenclature that is associated with these rituals, such as "Agni Hotra" (a fire sacrifice dedicated to Agni, the god of fire), "Soma Yajna" (a sacrifice involving the ritualistic use of the hallucinogenic plant soma), and "Ashvamedha" (a horse sacrifice), reflects the ritualistic practices that were prevalent during the Vedic period. Not only do these names bring attention to the religious significance of the rites, but they also make a contribution to the lexicon that is linked with religious ceremonies in the larger Indian culture.

Transitions in Nomenclature and Their Continuity and Development:

The development of Vedic terminology:

During the transition from the Vedic period to following ages, the name of the region went through a process of change. The names and words that were first employed during the Vedic period continued to be utilized and changed in a variety of various circumstances all throughout history. This development of the region's nomenclature was further contributed to by the epics, such as the Mahabharata and the Ramayana, which introduced new characters, places, and events to the region's lexicon.

As an illustration, the name "Ayodhya," which refers to the fabled city that is associated with the Ramayana, evolved into not only a geographical identification but also a symbol of cultural and religious significance. In a similar vein, the city of "Dwaraka," which is mentioned in the Mahabharata and is associated with Lord Krishna, continues to be of great spiritual significance.

Diversities in Regional and Linguistic Communities:

Despite the fact that the Vedic period was responsible for laying the groundwork for the region's language, the ensuing centuries saw the development of a number of different linguistic families and regional spoken languages. The fusion of linguistic influences, each of which contributes to the regional nomenclature, is reflected in the diverse linguistic landscape that India possesses.

While regional languages such as Tamil, Telugu, Kannada, and Malayalam grew in various parts of the subcontinent, Sanskrit, which is considered to be a classical language, continued to serve as a medium for the expression of literary and philosophical ideas. Each language heritage contributed its own unique collection of names, which contributed to the diverse and intricate nomenclature of the region.

The Vedic period, with its linguistic accomplishments, cultural manifestations, and religious fervor, was a significant contributor to the formation of the nomenclature of the Indian subcontinent. There is a connection between modern-day India and its ancient origins through the names of rivers, mountains, cities, and deities that are described in the Vedas. These names continue to reverberate down the corridors of time.

The contributions to language that were made during the Vedic period, in particular the improvement of Sanskrit, served as a common thread that was used to weave together a variety of linguistic traditions. The cultural and religious terminology that was established in the Vedic hymns, rituals, and philosophical discourses eventually formed fundamental components of the identity of the region.

As the Indian subcontinent advanced through following historical epochs, the nomenclature developed, reflecting the dynamic nature of a civilization that was in a state of perpetual upheaval. The names that are linked with the Vedic period continue to resound, whether they are in reference to geographical features, deities, or ceremonial practices. This helps to maintain a sense of continuity and cultural connectivity. In this manner, the influence of the Vedic period on the nomenclature of the region extends beyond the confines of time, providing a comprehensive understanding of the ongoing legacy of ancient India.

3.2 Examination of Sanskrit literature and its influence on naming conventions

One of the world's oldest and most sophisticated literary traditions, Sanskrit literature has had a significant impact on the cultural, religious, and linguistic landscape of the Indian subcontinent. It is one of the literary traditions that has been passed down from generation to generation. Sanskrit, which is the language of the sacred writings, philosophical treatises, epics, and classical poetry, has not only been responsible for the preservation of the intellectual and cultural heritage of ancient India, but it has also had a considerable impact on the naming practices that are used in the region. In the course of this investigation, we delve into the various domains of Sanskrit literature and investigate the influence that it has had on the naming of people, places, deities, and cultural conceptions.

A General Introduction to Sanskrit Literature

The Brahmanas and the Vedas:

In Sanskrit literature, the Vedas, which are considered to be the most ancient sacred scriptures in Hinduism, serve as the fundamental corpus. This collection of writings includes the Rigveda, Samaveda, Yajurveda, and Atharvaveda, all of which were written during the Vedic period. It was the hymns, ceremonies, and philosophical theories that were included in the Vedas that laid the groundwork for the eventual development of Sanskrit literature.

Following in the footsteps of the Vedas, the Brahmanas are a collection of prose works that are coupled with ritualistic explanations and commentary. They go into greater depth on the significance of rites and provide instructions that are very specific regarding ceremonies and sacrifices. Using their complicated language frameworks, the Brahmanas made additional contributions to the development of Sanskrit and provided the groundwork for the philosophical and literary traditions that came later.

Upanishads:

The Upanishads, which are believed to be the conclusion of Vedic thinking, are known for their profound philosophical questions regarding the nature of existence, the self, and the ultimate truth (Brahman). The move from ritualistic rituals to contemplative and speculative philosophy is marked by these works, which are frequently presented in the form of dialogues between instructors and students.

The naming conventions that are connected with metaphysical and philosophical topics were substantially affected by the Upanishads through their widespread popularity.

Words like "Atman" (which means "the individual soul"), "Brahman" (which means "the ultimate reality"), and "Moksha" (which means "liberation") that were discovered in the Upanishads eventually became essential components of the Sanskrit lexicon. These words not only influenced the discourse from the religious perspective, but also the wider cultural and intellectual environment.

Epics, including the Mahabharata and the Ramayana:

Both the Mahabharata and the Ramayana are considered to be among the most significant literary accomplishments in Sanskrit literature during this time period. The Mahabharata is an epic story that is said to have been written by the wise master Vyasa. It contains the Bhagavad Gita, which is a philosophical conversation that takes place between Lord Krishna and the warrior Arjuna. The life and exploits of Lord Rama are recounted in the Ramayana, which is a work that is attributed to the wise man Valmiki.

Conventions of naming have been profoundly influenced by these epics, which have resulted in the introduction of a multitude of names for characters, locations, and ideas. In Indian cultural consciousness, the names of heroic figures such as Arjuna, Yudhishthira, Rama, Sita, and Hanuman have become synonymous with the concept of legendary figures. In addition, the epic narratives have made a contribution to the lexicon that is linked with moral and ethical conundrums, the dynamics of the family, and the cosmic conflict between good and evil.

Puranas

The Puranas are a type of ancient Indian literature that are encyclopedic in form. They contain storylines that are mythological, cosmological, and genealogical in nature. The Vishnu Purana, the Shiva Purana, and the Bhagavata Purana are only some of the books that are included in these works. They have been extremely important in the dissemination of religious knowledge and tales.

The name practices that are linked with deities, celestial creatures, and sacred sites have been profoundly impacted by the Puranas by a significant amount. Some of the names that may be found in the Puranas, such as Vishnu, Shiva, Lakshmi, Parvati, and Brahma, have become an essential part of the lexicon used in Hindu religious practices. The Puranic narratives, on the other hand, frequently entail the personification of abstract notions, which leads to the development of names that embody various aspects of the cosmic order and mythology.

The Impact on the Conventions Regarding Naming

Personal Names:

Literature written in Sanskrit has had a significant role in the development of the practice of naming individuals in Indian civilization. There is a strong correlation between personal names and cultural, religious, or familial values, and a significant number of these names have their origins in Sanskrit compositions. The names of gods, goddesses, and other people from mythology are frequently employed as personal names, which endows individuals with a connection to their religious and cultural past.

As an illustration, names like Sita, Lakshmi, Arjuna, and Rama are widely used throughout India, and their roots may be traced back to the Ramayana and the Mahabharata. Not only do these names have grammatical and aesthetic appeal, but they also have a cultural resonance that connects individuals to the diverse literary traditions that are woven into the fabric of Sanskrit.

Names of the Places:

The names of locations and physical features are clear examples of the influence that Sanskrit literature has had on the world. Names that have their origins in Sanskrit are frequently given to cities, towns, rivers, and mountains. These names sometimes imply a connection to religious, mythical, or historical narratives. The Puranas, the Vedas, and the epics have all made significant contributions to the development of a diversified geographical nomenclature that encapsulates the impact of culture.

One example is the city of Varanasi, which was named after the point where the Varuna and Assi rivers meet. The mention of this city may be found in ancient manuscripts. In a similar vein, the name Ayodhya, which is connected to the Ramayana, is a symbol of a city that cannot be invaded, highlighting the city's sacred and legendary significance.

Names of the Deities:

The name traditions that are linked with religious practices have been profoundly influenced by the pantheon of Hindu deities, which is documented in Sanskrit literature. People who are devoted to a particular deity frequently select names for their children that are derived from the characteristics, features, or stories associated with that deity.

Names such as Krishna, Radha, Shiva, Parvati, and Sarasvati are among the most popular choices, and they are derived from the extensive body of Sanskrit literature.

In addition to having religious importance, these names also exemplify the aspirational values that are associated with the deities that they represent.

Conceptual Names:

The literature of Sanskrit has been responsible for the introduction of a great number of philosophical and conceptual concepts, many of which have made their way into naming conventions. Dharma, which means "righteousness," Karma, which means "action," Yoga, which means "union," and Moksha, which means "liberation," are all examples of abstract principles that have become essential components of both human and geographical names.

For example, the name Dharmanand is linked with the idea of living one's life in accordance with the principles of Dharma, whereas the name Yogesh is associated with a person who is involved in spiritual practices. Not only can these conceptual names convey a profound philosophical understanding, but they also add to the linguistic diversity that exists within naming conventions.

Literature in Sanskrit and the Maintenance of Cultural Continuity
Preserving the Cultural Heritage of the Community:

The cultural heritage of ancient India has been preserved and passed down through generations thanks in large part to the contributions of Sanskrit literature. Through their hymns and rites, the Vedas are able to encompass the social and religious activities that were prevalent during the Vedic period. The Mahabharata and the Ramayana are two of the most famous Indian epics, and they tell stories of heroic deeds, moral conundrums, and cosmic struggles that continue to have an imprint on modern Indian society.

Name conventions that can be found in Sanskrit literature are examples of linguistic artifacts that assist to bridge the gap between the present and the past. Individuals and locations are able to take part in a cultural continuity that is not limited by the constraints of time when they use names that are drawn from historically significant writings.

Elements of Culture That Bring Together:

Because of the diverse range of genres and topics that it covers, Sanskrit literature has served as a cultural force that has brought people together across the Indian subcontinent. Sanskrit-based names give a common cultural thread that connects together a variety of communities, despite the fact that these cultures are linguistically and geographically distinct from one another.

The sense of cultural cohesion that is created is a result of the shared familiarity with characters, stories, and concepts that are found in Sanskrit literature. Whether it be in the naming of festivals, rituals, or personalities, the influence of Sanskrit literature helps to promote a sense of cultural unity that transcends the limits of both language and place.

The Obstacles and Adjustments to Overcome

Globalization and the Process of Modernization:
During the modern age, which is characterized by modernity and globalization, name traditions in India have undergone alterations. Despite the fact that names derived from Sanskrit continue to be popular, there is also a growing tendency toward adopting names from other linguistic traditions or developing hybrid names that combine characteristics of both traditional and contemporary names.

It is a reflection of the changing cultural dynamics as well as the influence of global trends that this difference has occurred. The adaptability of naming conventions in response to shifting social, cultural, and linguistic environments is brought to light by this.

Diversity in Regional and Linguistic Perspectives:
The fact that India is home to a large number of languages and dialects is evidence of the country's significant linguistic diversity. In the process of naming conventions, every language tradition makes a contribution by contributing distinctive sounds, phonetics, and characteristics of meaning.

Numerous regional languages and dialects have also contributed to the formation of the naming practices, which has resulted in a nomenclature that is both diverse and dynamic. Sanskrit has played a foundational role in this process. The cultural fabric of India is enriched with additional layers of linguistic richness as a result of the regionalization of names.

The naming practices of the Indian subcontinent have been irrevocably altered as a result of the widespread and diverse corpus of Sanskrit literature. There is little doubt that Sanskrit literature has had a profound and everlasting impact on a wide range of topics, from human names to place names, and from conceptual concepts to deities.

Beyond the realm of language aesthetics, the resonance of names that are derived from Sanskrit literature is significant. Through this, people and communities are able to establish a connection to a cultural history that spans millennia.

The ageless tales, philosophical truths, and linguistic intricacies that are inherent in Sanskrit literature continue to impact the way in which people name themselves, their children, and the locations that they inhabit.

It is a testament to the cultural continuity and resiliency of a culture that is strongly rooted in its literary and philosophical traditions that the effect of Sanskrit literature on naming practices continues to exist even as India navigates the challenges of the modern world. Not only do the names that originate from the worlds of Sanskrit literature serve as identifiers of identity, but they also act as threads that weave together the history, present, and future of the Indian subcontinent.

3.3 Insight into how regional names coexisted during this era
In ancient times, India was a land that was home to a wide variety of cultures, languages, and regions, all of which contributed to the intricately woven history of the subcontinent. The dynamic interplay of numerous linguistic, cultural, and political influences is reflected in the coexistence of regional names during this time period. Beginning with the Vedic period and continuing through the classical and

medieval times, India has been witness to the birth and coexistence of a myriad of regional names, each of which possesses its own distinct identity and was significant historically. In the course of this investigation, we delve into the historical backdrop of regional names in ancient India. We investigate the circumstances that contributed to the coexistence of these names, as well as the impact that this diversity had on the cultural and social fabric of the subcontinent.

The Vedic Period: A Versatile Approach to Naming Regulations

The diversity of languages:

As a result of the migration of numerous Indo-Aryan groups into the Indian sub-continent, the Vedic era, which lasted from around 1500 BCE to 500 BCE, was characterized by a wide range of linguistic varieties. Throughout the course of religious and philosophical discourse, the Vedas, which were written in Sanskrit, served as a uniting force. Despite this, regional dialects and languages coexisted alongside Sanskrit, which reflected the different origins of the people who spoke the Vedic language.

The Rigveda, for example, makes reference to a number of different clans and tribes, each of which has a unique identity and possibly speaks a different language. Within the larger Vedic civilization, the linguistic landscape was defined by the coexistence of a number of different Indo-Aryan dialects, each of which contributed to the regional diversity that existed within the region.

Regional Entities:

The later Vedic period saw the emergence of permanent agricultural communities, which led to the formation of regional units that possessed distinct cultural traits. The formation of the Mahajanapadas, also known as the great kingdoms, signified a change from the nomadic way of life of the early Vedic people to the construction of territorial states. The Mahajanapadas each had their own distinct identity, language, and system of governance, which contributed to the patchwork of regional names that existed in ancient India.

It was through the establishment of kingdoms like Magadha, Kuru, and Kosala that the multiplicity of regional entities that coexisted within the Vedic cultural framework was brought to light. Epic stories from this time period, such as the Mahabharata and the Ramayana, offer insights into the political and social climate of the time, which was characterized by the significant importance that regional names played in determining individuals' identities.

During the Classical Era, regional governments and cultural flourishing were prevalent

Political Disparities and Divisions:

The establishment of major empires and provincial policies occurred during the classical age, which generally lasted from the fourth century BCE to the sixth century CE after the common era. A considerable political consolidation occurred during the Maurya Empire, which was established by Chandragupta Maurya in the fourth century BCE. However, the Maurya Empire also witnessed the preservation of regional identities within the greater frame of the imperial framework.

The Mauryan Empire exercised political authority over a huge realm that encompassed a variety of regions, each of which had its own distinct culture and language. Despite the fact that the imperial administration was run in a centralized fashion, local governance mechanisms made it possible for regional names and identities to continue to exist. After then, the Gupta Empire continued a pattern of political fragmentation that was very similar to the previous one, with regional entities establishing their power across the empire.

Relatively Rich Cultural Life:

There was a time of cultural prosperity known as the classical age, which was characterized by great developments in the fields of literature, art, and philosophy. Classical Sanskrit literature, which includes works such as the dramas of Kalidasa, the Arthashastra, which is attributed to Chanakya, and the philosophical treatises known as the Sutras, contributed to the cultural diversity that existed throughout that time period.

Literary works that honored the distinctive identities of many regions provided a creative outlet for the expression of regional names. In his works, Kalidasa, who is frequently referred to as the "Shakespeare of India," created depictions that highlighted the aesthetic appeal and cultural uniqueness of locations such as Ujjain. In addition, the Sanskrit drama "Mricchakatika" by Shudraka offers insights into regional variations, bringing attention to the coexistence of a variety of ethnicities.

The Middle Ages: The Emergence of Regional Kingdoms and the Syncretism Movement

Kingdoms in the Provinces:

The establishment of powerful regional kingdoms in India occurred throughout the medieval period, which roughly covered the time span from the sixth to the eighteenth century. In the sixth century, the Gupta Empire began to disintegrate, which resulted in the establishment of regional empires such as the Chalukyas, Pallavas, and Cholas in the southern region, and the Harsha Empire in the northern region. In order to facilitate the consolidation of regional identities, the decentralization of political power was implemented.

At the time, the Rashtrakutas, Chalukyas, and Hoysalas were all competing for control in the Deccan region. Each of these three families contributed to the cultural diversity that exists on the subcontinent. Additional examples of the presence of different political entities during this time period can be found in the Rajput kingdoms that were located in the northern region. These kingdoms had separate regional identities.

The theory of cultural syncretism

During the medieval time, there was also a phenomenon known as cultural syncretism, which was defined by the coexistence of various religious and cultural traditions that in turn impacted one another. The spread of Islam throughout India during the medieval period resulted in the establishment of the Delhi Sultanate, which brought to the forefront regional names such as the Tughlaqs and the Khiljis. A distinctive

Indo-Islamic cultural identity emerged as a result of the combination of indigenous civilizations and Islamic influences from around the world.

The Bhakti and Sufi groups, both of which rose to prominence during this time period, were instrumental in the development of a common spiritual lexicon that moved beyond the confines of certain regions. The diversity of linguistic and cultural manifestations is reflected in the fact that poets such as Kabir and Sant Tukaram conveyed their devotion in vernacular languages while writing their poems.

The Mughal Empire: A Unified Government and the Independence of Its Regions

Rule That Is Centralized:

In 1526, Babur established the Mughal Empire, which was a period of time that was characterized by centralized rule over a broad territory. The Mughals was responsible for establishing a powerful imperial administration that encompassed the Deccan region as well as the northern plains. Despite the fact that they maintained a centralized authority, the Mughal emperors understood the significance of regional autonomy.

The appointment of provincial governors, who were referred to as Subahdars, to oversee various regions made it possible for a certain degree of local authority to exist. The art, architecture, and language of the Mughal court were all influenced by the Mughals' incorporation of numerous regional components into their courtling culture. Within the context of Mughal administration, the coexistence of regional names signified an acceptance of the cultural diversity that existed across the subcontinent.

Autonomy among the Regions:

Although the Mughals maintained a centralized rule, regional autonomy continued to flourish throughout their reign. A degree of self-rule was maintained by the Rajput states in Rajasthan, for instance, even though they were subject to Mughal suzerainty. Under the leadership of influential figures such as Chhatrapati Shivaji, the Marathas in western India established an area that was known as the Maratha Confederacy. This region was a semi-autonomous region.

The decline of the Mughal Empire in the 18th century coincided with the establishment of autonomous regional entities, which marked the beginning of a new period in the history of India. The regional names that were linked with these groups were a reflection of the continued coexistence of a variety of identities within the subcontinent.

During the time of British colonial rule, regional diversity and linguistic reckoning

The British Raj and the Divisions of Administrative Power:

During the time period of British colonial rule in India, which lasted from the 18th century until 1947, a crucial period in the subcontinent's history occurred. A new administrative structure was established as a result of the expansion of the British East India Company and the subsequent consolidation of direct authority by the British crown.

Within the framework of the British Raj, territories were divided into provinces, presidencies, and princely states, each of which had its own administrative composition. Due to the fact that the British acknowledged the considerable linguistic and cultural diversity that existed on the subcontinent, the coexistence of regional names continued to exist within this administrative framework.

Linguistic Reckoning

Additionally, during the time of colonial rule, there was a rising awareness of linguistic identities taking place. The British government was motivated to establish language-based administrative divisions in India due to the country's diverse linguistic landscape. It was an endeavor to connect administrative entities with linguistic regions that led to the construction of linguistic provinces. One example of this is the foundation of the province of Bengal in 1905, which was followed by its reorganization in 1911.

Following the attainment of independence, the linguistic rearrangement of provinces grew increasingly evident, culminating in the establishment of states based on language identity in the year 1956. The significance of regional languages in determining cultural and linguistic identities was acknowledged through this process, which showed the recognition of the issue.

States Based on Linguistic Identity During the Post-Independence Era and After Independence

State of the Linguistic Art:

In India, the period following the country's independence was marked by the rearrangement of states according to their linguistic identities. This marked a substantial break from the administrative divisions that existed beneath British administration. The linguistic reorganization, which was carried out in 1956, had the objective of establishing states that were in accordance with the most prominent language groupings in the country.

A number of states, including Maharashtra, Gujarat, Tamil Nadu, and West Bengal, were established as a result of the States Reorganization Act. These states are representations of the linguistic and cultural variety that exists within the territories. This rearrangement made it possible for a wider number of language and regional identities to be represented in decisions regarding governance.

Federal Structure:

Within the context of the larger political framework, India selected a federal structure that included both states and union territories.

This structure allowed for higher levels of regional autonomy. In addition to enshrining the ideals of equality and non-discrimination, the Constitution of India acknowledges the linguistic and cultural variety that exists inside the country.

There is a clear indication of the coexistence of regional names in the numerous states and union territories, each of which possesses its own distinct personality and cultural legacy. A platform that allows for the expression and maintenance of regional variation within the framework of the Indian nation's united structure is provided by the federal structure.

Impact on Culture and Contemporary Perspectives
Social Integration and the Diversity of Cultures:

There was a significant influence on the cultural variety and integration of the subcontinent as a result of the coexistence of regional names in ancient India. The interaction of various linguistic, religious, and cultural traditions has resulted in the creation of a cultural tapestry that is both rich and unique in its diversity.

The distinct identities that have been cultivated over the course of centuries are reflected in the cultural activities, festivals, art forms, and language expressions that vary from place to region. While this is going on, the shared history, syncretic traditions, and cultural aspects that overlap all contribute to a feeling of national identity that is not limited by geographical limits.

Perspectives on Things in the Present:

Within the context of modern-day India, the coexistence of regional names is not just a manifestation of historical legacies, but it is also a dynamic component of the ever-evolving national identity. A key component of India's pluralistic culture is the acknowledgment and celebration of the country's linguistic and regional variety.

There are many different fields in which regional identities can be expressed, such as in the fields of literature, film, music, and gastronomy. The historical and cultural origins of a region are frequently reflected in the naming of cities, landmarks, and organizations originating from that region. In India, the coexistence of regional names is cherished as an essential component of the country's identity, which contributes to the nation's vitality and dynamism.

A monument to the varied and ever-changing history of the subcontinent is the fact that regional names coexisted in ancient India.

Beginning with the Vedic period and continuing up till the present day, the interaction of linguistic, cultural, and political forces has resulted in the formation of a mosaic of identities that continue to coexist within the wider overall framework of the Indian nation.

The acknowledgment and preservation of regional names have made a significant contribution to the cultural wealth, linguistic diversity, and historical continuity that India possesses. Despite the fact that diverse regions have been ruled by empires, kingdoms, and colonial powers throughout history, the distinct identities that are connected with those locations have not been eradicated. Instead, they have added levels of richness and delicacy to the coexistence of regional names, producing a tapestry that represents the unity in diversity that constitutes the heart of India. Despite the fact that the subcontinent is navigating the challenges and opportunities of the 21st century, the coexistence of regional names continues to be a living monument to the resiliency, adaptation, and cultural vitality of Indian civilization.

Chapter 4

The Mughal Influence

The Mughal Empire, which originated in the early 16th century and lasted until the middle of the 19th century, is often regarded as one of the most influential and iconic empires in the history of India. In 1526, Babur established the Mughal empire, which left an unmistakable impact on the Indian subcontinent. The Mughals were responsible for molding the political, cultural, artistic, and architectural landscape of the region. This in-depth investigation dives into the myriad of facets that comprise the Mughal influence. It investigates the impact that the Mughal empire had on governance, society, art, architecture, and religion, as well as the lingering legacy that continues to exist in modern-day India.

The establishment of the Mughal Empire

Conquest of Babur:

Babur, who was a descendant of Timur on his father's side and Genghis Khan on his mother's side, is the single most important figure in the history of the Mughal Empire. Following the loss of his dominion in Central Asia, Babur shifted his focus to India on the continent. During the Battle of Panipat, which took place in 1526, he achieved a major victory over Ibrahim Lodhi, the Sultan of Delhi, and laid the groundwork for the establishment of the Mughal Federation. The establishment of this dynasty heralded the beginning of a period that would have a profound impact on the development of Indian history.

Akbar, the Great Khan:

In the annals of Mughal Empire history, Akbar, the grandson of Babur, is frequently considered to be among the most influential and influential kings. His reign, which lasted from 1556 until 1605, was marked by political consolidation, administrative reforms, and endeavors to unify a variety of religions and civilizations. The policies that Akbar implemented, which came to be known as the "Akbari system," were designed to promote religious tolerance, meritocracy, and effective governance.

The implementation of a centralized administrative structure, which came to be known as the Mansabdari system, made it possible to appoint officials in a manner that was both more effective and more justified by merit. In addition, Akbar's policies included the elimination of the Jizya tax, which was levied on non-Muslims, the development of a syncretic culture known as Din-i Ilahi, and the establishment of a rich cultural and intellectual milieu within his court.

Innovations in Governance and Administrative Procedures

Mansabdari System:

During the time of the Mughal Empire, Akbar established the Mansabdari system, which is considered to be one of the most significant administrative improvements. Every officer, whether they were in the military or the civil service, was assigned a rank that was referred to as "mansab." It was the official's rank that controlled both the amount of money he was paid and the number of soldiers he was obliged to keep for imperial service. A merit-based approach to appointment scheduling was made possible by this method, which also ensured that the bureaucracy was both professional and loyal.

System of Revenue:

In addition to this, Akbar made significant changes to the way the revenue system worked. The old method of tax collection, which was referred to as the Zabt system, was succeeded by the Todar Mal's system, which included the objective of determining the level of agricultural productivity. This revenue system, which was a change from the earlier arbitrary assessment and helped to more equitable taxation, was based on actual measurements of the production of land and crops.

In the case of tolerance and syncretism:

In contrast to the prevalent practice of the period, Akbar's policy of religious tolerance was a radical change. He aimed to establish a society that was a synthesis of several religions and transcendent religious borders. Akbar's dedication to promoting religious unity was demonstrated by the creation of the Ibadat Khana (House of Worship) in Fatehpur Sikri. This house served as a gathering place for academics of many religions to participate in discourse.

The Din-i Ilahi was a syncretic faith that took influence from a variety of religions. It was the outcome of Akbar's efforts to merge numerous religious ideas. Akbar's willingness to embrace a wide variety of religious traditions had a significant and long-lasting effect on the cultural and social fabric of the Mughal Empire, despite the fact that the Din-i Ilahi did not receive popular support.

The Society and Culture of the Mughals

The arts and architecture:

Particularly in the fields of art and architecture, the Mughal era is recognized for its abundance of cultural and artistic accomplishments, which are particularly noteworthy.

During the reign of Akbar, the Mughal school of painting flourished. This school of painting was distinguished by its detailed details, brilliant colors, and a combination of Persian and Indian artistic forms.

The construction of Fatehpur Sikri, a city that was created by Akbar, and the well-known Agra Fort are both instances of notable examples of Mughal architecture. On the other hand, the Taj Mahal, which is considered to be the most recognizable example of Mughal architecture, was constructed during the reign of Shah Jahan, Akbar's grandson. A monument to the Mughals' mastery of architectural aesthetics and their ability to merge multiple elements into a harmonious whole, the Taj Mahal is a building that stands as a testament to both this talent.

The realms of literature and language:

A flowering of writing in Persian, which was the court language of the Mughals, was one of the defining characteristics of the Mughal era. To be more specific, Akbar was a supporter of Persian literature and endeavored to establish a cultural synthesis that would mix the literary traditions of Persian literature with the languages of indigenous Indian regions. The Persian language evolved into a medium through which the culture of the Mughal court could be expressed. During this time period, a great number of historical chronicles and literary works were written.

Lifestyle and the Food You Eat:

Additionally, the Mughals played a significant role in the development of India's well-known culinary traditions. Mughlai cuisine is the outcome of a synthesis of several different culinary styles, including those from India, Central Asia, and Persian influences. The rich and distinctive culinary history of the Mughal era, which continues to influence Indian cuisine to this day, is reflected in many dishes, including biryani, kebabs, and curries.

In addition to their influence on cuisine, the Mughals also left their mark on lifestyle and dressing styles. The Mughals had a significant impact on the aesthetics of everyday life, as seen by the introduction of the Anarkali-style attire, the use of exquisite textiles, and the usage of extravagant jewels.

The Influence on the Economy and Trade

Economy Based on Agriculture:

The economic landscape of India was significantly altered as a result of the expansion of the Mughal Empire. Agriculture was the principal source of money for the empire, and the agrarian economy served as the foundation of the empire.

In the manner that it was reformed by Akbar, the revenue system was designed to ensure that agricultural productivity was evaluated fairly and that taxation was distributed fairly.

In addition to the development of core food crops, the introduction of cash crops such as cotton and indigo was a significant contributor to the economic prosperity of the Mughal Empire. Because of the effective system for collecting income, a big and well-paid bureaucracy was able to be maintained, which contributed to the maintenance of economic stability.

Business & Commercial Transactions:

Trade and commerce on a massive scale were made easier by the Mughal Empire's geographical location, which allowed for their expansion. During its time, the empire served as a hub for the trade of goods, ideas, and cultural practices. It was during the time of the Mughals that the Grand Trunk Road was constructed. This road connected key cities and trading areas, making it easier for people and products to move both ways.

Attracting merchants from all over the known globe, cities such as Agra, Delhi, and Lahore developed into thriving hubs of trade and commerce. The Mughals were involved in commerce with European powers such as the Portuguese, Dutch, and British, which resulted in the construction of European trading stations in India thanks to their activities.

Craftsmanship and artisanal arts and crafts:

During the time of the Mughals, a wide variety of crafts and activities that involve artisanal work flourished. Highly skilled artisans were responsible for the production of magnificent commodities like fabrics, carpets, pottery, and metalwork. Craftsmanship of exceptional quality was produced as a result of the patronage of the Mughal monarchs and the incorporation of a wide range of artistic influences. This resulted in the development of works that had widespread recognition both within and beyond the empire.

The Policies of Religion and Their Legacy

Pluralism in Religious Practices:

In spite of the fact that they were of Turko-Mongol and Timurid heritage, the Mughals were recognized for their policy of tolerance and their acceptance of religious heterogeneity. A specific focus of Akbar's administration was the implementation of programs that were designed to promote unity among various religious sects. His involvement with experts from a variety of religious traditions and his decision to do away with the Jizya tax that was levied on non-Muslims were both examples of his dedication to peaceful tolerance across different faiths.

It is well known that the Mughal kings, such as Akbar, Jahangir, and Shah Jahan, were noted for their support of a variety of religious organizations. In the Mughal era, temples, mosques, and churches were all given sponsorship by the imperial government, which contributed to the cultural fusion that was characteristic of that time period.

Architects of Religious Buildings:

The Mughals left an indelible impact on the field of religious architecture by erecting magnificent monuments that displayed the myriad of religious influences that were present at the time. The Taj Mahal is a monument to Islamic architecture, but the Akshardham Temple in Delhi and the Golden Temple in Amritsar are examples of the Mughals' encouragement of Hindu and Sikh religious structures, respectively. Both of these temples are notable for their architectural design.

As a result of the Mughals' dedication to the creation of spaces that transcended religious borders, the architectural legacy that they left behind exemplifies the syncretic ethos that was prevalent across the empire. The enduring emblems of religious tolerance and cultural integration that these structures represent are the structures themselves.

Decline in the Harmony of Religious Practices:

More specifically, during the reign of Aurangzeb, the Mughal Empire experienced a deterioration in religious peace throughout the later years of its existence. Religion-related tensions were exacerbated as a result of his actions, which included the reinstatement of the Jizya tax, the destruction of specific temples, and the prohibition of behaviors that were not associated with the Muslim faith.

There was dissatisfaction among a number of different religious sects as a result of Aurangzeb's rigorous approach to government and his attempts to impose a more orthodox view of Islam. During the latter Mughal period, there was a collapse in religious peace, which paved the way for social and political issues that would eventually contribute to the decline of the empire.

The Fall and the Legacy

Instability in the Political System:

The decline of the Mughal Empire was characterized by a number of elements, including governmental instability, internal disputes, and external invasions. These developments occurred simultaneously. The slow decline of Mughal authority as a result of successive weak emperors, the formation of regional forces, and the encroachment of European colonial powers were all factors that contributed to the decline of Mughal authority.

The empire suffered serious blows as a result of the invasions of Nadir Shah in 1739 and Ahmad Shah Durrani in 1761. These invasions led to the looting of Delhi as well as the ruin of its wealth and infrastructure. The subsequent internal struggle and the existence of independent regional states both contributed to the acceleration of the decline of the Mughal Empire.

The Legacy of Artistic and Cultural Values:

In spite of the demise of the Mughal Empire's governmental power, the cultural and artistic legacy of the empire persisted. It was during the Mughal era that India's cultural landscape was shaped by the architectural marvels, literary successes, and creative advances that were created during that time period. Particularly noteworthy is the Taj Mahal, which serves as a representation of everlasting love and masterful architectural design.

As a result of its synthesis of Persian and Indian forms, the Mughal school of painting had a significant impact on later artistic traditions. Mughal cuisine, which is a combination of a wide range of different culinary traditions, continues to be an essential component of Indian food. The legacy of the Mughals extends to the realm of language as well, with Persian continuing to exert an effect on Indian cultures and literature.

Effects on Governance:

The administrative improvements that were implemented by the Mughals, such as the Mansabdari system and revenue reforms, had a significant and long-lasting effect on the governance of India. The idea of a centralized bureaucratic system, appointments based on merit, and income assessment based on productivity were all concepts that inspired succeeding rulers and administrations.

The Mughal administration was responsible for the establishment of administrative systems that contributed to the construction of a framework that was capable of being adapted and modified by subsequent rulers, including the administration of the British colonial government.

Historical remembrance and personal identity:

There is little doubt that the Mughals continue to have a crucial position in the historical memory and identity of India. India's history narrative will not be complete without mentioning the cultural syncretism that was encouraged by the Mughal kings, the architectural accomplishments that they accomplished, and the influence that they had on the economic and social fabric of the subcontinent.

On the other hand, the remembrance of the Mughals is both complicated and multifaceted, with discussions and contrasting viewpoints regarding their legacy.

Although there are those who believe that the Mughals were responsible for the cultural diversity and pluralistic ethos that exists in India, there are also those who highlight the disputes and religious tensions that were prevalent throughout specific times of Mughal administration.

Recent Perspectives on the Situation

Tourism and the heritage of cultural arts:

The legacy of the Mughals is a significant component of India's cultural heritage, and it is responsible for the influx of millions of tourists to internationally renowned destinations like the Taj Mahal, Agra Fort, and Fatehpur Sikri. These monuments, which have been designated as UNESCO World Heritage sites, make a substantial contribution to India's tourism economy and serve as emblems of the country's extensive historical and architectural heritage.

Debates Regarding the Past:

Discussions about the Mughal Empire's influence on Indian society and identity are frequently a topic of contention among contemporary opinions on the empire. There are many problems that scholars and historians are trying to answer, including those concerning religious tolerance, cultural synthesis, and the role that the Mughals played in defining the social and political environment of India. In addition, debates revolve around questions of historical representation and interpretation, with different narratives being presented depending on the ideological and cultural perspectives of the participants.

Traditions of Syncretic Sound:

Celebrating the Mughal legacy as an embodiment of syncretic traditions is something that continues to be doing now. The contributions that the Mughals made to a cultural environment that was diverse and welcoming are frequently used as a source of inspiration for festivals, literary events, and cultural gatherings. The syncretic ethos of the Mughals provides a counterweight to tales that divide people and encourages a respect for the heterogeneous identity of India.

The influence of the Mughals on India is a chapter in the history of the country that is composed of many different aspects and complexities. The influence of the Mughal empire may be seen in many different aspects of Indian life, from its beginnings with Babur's conquest to the architectural marvels of Akbar, Jahangir, and Shah Jahan, as well as the cultural synthesis that was characteristic of the Mughal era.

An enduring legacy has been left behind by the Mughals as a result of their contributions to subjects like governance, society, art, architecture, and religious tolerance.

Although the fall of the empire brought about a change in the political dynamics of the world, the cultural and artistic accomplishments of the Mughals continue to have a significant impact on India's identity as well as how the rest of the world views its extensive past.

It is a monument to the Mughals' ongoing influence that contemporary India is a testament to the Mughals' architectural wonders, artistic traditions, and syncretic ethos, all of which contribute to the vivid tapestry that is India. The Mughal era continues to be an essential component of India's historical narrative, and it is therefore worthy of further investigation, interpretation, and appreciation due to the enormous and long-lasting impact it had on the territory of the subcontinent.

4.1 Exploration of the Mughal era and its impact on language and nomenclature

During the Mughal era in India, which began in the early 16th century and lasted until the middle of the 19th century, there was a period of enormous cultural, political, and linguistic change. A significant contribution to the formation of linguistic traditions and nomenclature on the Indian subcontinent was made by the Mughal kings, who were renowned for their generous support of the arts and their efforts to establish a culture that was a syncretic heritage. This investigation dives into the linguistic landscape of the Mughal Empire, including an examination of the influence of the empire on languages, naming customs, and the legacy that continues to exist in modern-day India.

The Presence of Multiple Languages Within the Mughal Empire
Empire of Multiple Languages:

It was a huge and diverse entity that comprised territories with different language traditions. The Mughal Empire was a vast and diverse entity. Turko-Mongols who spoke Chagatai Turkish were the rulers and aristocracy of the empire. Persian was the official language of government and culture, while Turko-Mongols spoke Chagatai Turkish. The Mughal Empire, on the other hand, encompassed expansive territories that were home to a diverse array of languages, such as Hindi, Bengali, Punjabi, Gujarati, and a number of others.

Central Asia, Persia, and the Indian subcontinent all contributed to the linguistic diversity that existed inside the empire. This diversity was a reflection of the fusion of many language traditions. Because of this linguistic diversity, a multicultural environment was created, in which a variety of languages coexisted and affected one another.

Persian as the Language Worn in the Court:

In spite of the fact that there were many different languages spoken, Persian was prioritized as the language spoken in the court of the Mughal Empire. Persian, with its extensive literary and cultural legacy, became the medium through which the Mughal monarchs interacted with their officials, conducted administrative business, and patronized the arts. Persian was also the language that was used to conduct administrative affairs.

Persian literature was supported by the Mughal rulers, including Akbar, Jahangir, and Shah Jahan, among others. Persian court poets contributed to the creation of a distinctive Indo-Persian literary heritage by writing ghazals, qasidas, and historical chronicles in the language of Persian.

The transformation of Indian languages into Persian

Impact on Knowledge of Vocabulary:

It had a significant influence on the lexicon of Indian languages as a result of Persian's preeminent position as the court language. A linguistic fusion that resulted in an enrichment of the linguistic landscape of the subcontinent was brought about by the incorporation of Persian loanwords and expressions into the lexicons of their respective regional languages.

The influence of Persian terminology is most noticeable in fields that are associated with administration and governance, as well as art, culture, industry, and commerce. In the context of government offices, titles, and administrative responsibilities, Persian elements were frequently incorporated into terms, resulting in the formation of a hybrid linguistic environment that mirrored the cultural synthesis of the Mughal administration.

Influence on Literature:

Courtly poetry was not the only kind of writing that was impacted by Persian literary traditions; vernacular literature in India's regional languages was also influenced. Poets writing in regional languages were inspired to adopt and incorporate Persian poetic forms and topics as a result of the Mughal monarchs' love of Persian poetry.

The Mughal era witnessed the creation of literary traditions that were Persianized in regional languages like Urdu, which arose as a distinct language during this time period. The syncretic structure of Urdu, which combines parts of Persian and local languages, is a reflection of the cultural and linguistic contacts that were made possible by the Mughal Empire.

The Urdu Language: A Linguistic Heritage of the Mughal Empire

The Emergence and Development of:

Urdu emerged as a unique literary and linguistic tradition during the Mughal era, which played a significant role in the evolution of the language to its current state. The Mughal courts and urban centers were essential in the development of Urdu as a language of cultural synthesis. Urdu is a language that originated from a combination of Persian, Turkish, Arabic, and local vernaculars.

Through their patronage of poets and intellectuals who authored in this burgeoning language, the Mughal kings and elites, who were fluent in multiple languages, made a significant contribution to the development of Urdu. In the Mughal courts, the interplay between Persian and indigenous languages resulted in the development of a distinct linguistic identity that would later flourish in the cultural environment of North India.

Influences on the Literary World:

Literary works written in Urdu flourished throughout the Mughal era. Poets such as Mir Taqi Mir, Sauda, and Siraj-ud-Din Ali Khan were among those who made significant contributions to the development of the language. The literary style known as the ghazal, which was initially popularized in Persian literature, discovered a new expression in Urdu poetry. The poets of the Mughal Empire drew influence from the literary traditions of Persian culture, which resulted in the infusion of Urdu poetry with elegance, beauty, and emotional depth.

The Mughal era left behind a literary heritage that established the groundwork for the development of Urdu as a language known for its poetry, culture, and expression. The syncretic aspect of Urdu, which bridges the linguistic and cultural divides between diverse communities, is a reflection of the role that the Mughals had in the development of a language that transcended not just religious boundaries but also regional divisions.

Nomenclature and Titles, Third Section
The Influence of Persian traditions on naming conventions:

In accordance with the cultural standards of the Persianate group, the Mughals adopted naming customs and titles that were founded in the traditions of the Persians. The linguistic and cultural characteristics of Persian were frequently reflected in the names of Mughal monarchs, princes, and other members of the Imperial Court. Babur, the founder of the Mughal Empire, for instance, had a name that was of Turkic origin; nevertheless, the titles that were bestowed upon him, such as "Padishah" (emperor), were Persian.

The practice of bestowing titles known as "takhallus" or "pen names" upon poets and intellectuals was another practice that adhered to Persian traditions. The use of poetic titles, which were frequently selected for their elegance and meaning, became a defining characteristic of the literary culture of the Mughal Empire.

Differentiations Across Regions:

There were regional variances that represented the linguistic diversity that existed within the empire, despite the fact that Persian seemed to have the most significant influence on naming customs. Throughout history, regional languages and dialects have continued to play an important part in the naming of individuals, places, and titles. The great diversity of name can be attributed, in part, to the incorporation of regional language aspects with Persian naming rules.

Akbar's policy of Sulh-i-kul, which translates to "peace with all," exemplifies how the Mughal kings encouraged linguistic and cultural diversity. This policy extended to the field of names and titles as well. This strategy, which was inclusive, helped to cultivate a sense of cultural unity throughout the empire, while simultaneously recognizing and enjoying the diversity of languages and customs that existed inside it.

The Influence on the Language and Culture of the Present Day

Influence that is still present:

It is clear that the Mughal era had a significant impact on both the language and culture of India in the modern day. In modern Indian languages, particularly Urdu, where a significant amount of the lexicon has Persian origins, the legacy of Persianized terminology continues to be present. The impact of Persian can also be seen in the names of cities, monuments, and cultural activities that are found all over the subcontinent.

Urdu as a Tradition That Does Not Die:

The linguistic syncretism that occurred during the Mughal dynasty gave rise to the language known as Urdu, which is still thriving as a live linguistic legacy. There is a rich literary and cultural tradition associated with it, and it is recognized as one of the official languages of both India and Pakistan. Urdu literature, which includes poetry, prose, and drama, continues to be an essential component of the cultural fabric of the Indian subcontinent.

The practice of embellishing official documents, poetry, and prose with beautiful calligraphy during the Mughal Empire was another factor that contributed to the aesthetic and artistic qualities of Urdu literature. There is a continued appreciation for this calligraphy heritage in current Urdu literature as well as visual arts.

Cultural Synthesis:

The theme of cultural synthesis encompasses the influence that the Mughal era had on language and nomenclature, which is interwoven within the larger concept. A cultural environment that transcended both regional and religious barriers was produced as a result of the mingling of components of Persian, Turkic, and Indian languages. This culture of syncretic creativity, which was characteristic of the Mughal Empire, continues to reverberate in the linguistic diversity and cultural wealth of the Indian subcontinent.

The Mughal era was a significant contributor to the formation of the linguistic and nomenclatural landscape of the Indian subcontinent. This was due to the Mughal era's linguistic diversity, cultural synthesis, and Persianate influences. As a monument to the Mughals' legacy of cultivating a syncretic and inclusive cultural attitude, the influence of Persian on Indian languages, in particular the formation of Urdu as a unique linguistic heritage, continues to be a significant factor.

The linguistic and cultural influences that were prevalent during the Mughal era have persisted through the intervening centuries, making a significant contribution to the rich tapestry of languages, literature, and naming conventions that exists in modern-day India. It is a reminder of the connectivity of various language traditions and the continuing strength of cultural synthesis that the legacy of the Mughal Empire continues to impact the linguistic and cultural identity of the subcontinent. This is because the Mughal Empire left behind a legacy that continues to shape the subcontinent.

4.2 Examination of how Persian influences shaped the linguistic landscape

One of the most fascinating chapters in the history of the Indian subcontinent is associated with the Persian effects that were exerted on the linguistic landscape of the region. A significant contribution to the formation of linguistic traditions was made during the Mughal era, which was distinguished by the use of Persian as the language of the court, the synthesis of cultural elements, and intellectual interactions. Within the scope of this investigation, the diverse impact of Persian on the linguistic landscape is investigated. Specifically, the influence of Persian on regional languages, naming customs, literature, and the persistent legacy that continues to exist in modern-day India is the subject of research.

The historical context: the arrival of Persians and their rise to power

Persian as the Language Worn in the Court:

Persian was brought to the Indian subcontinent during the early medieval period by the Ghaznavid and Ghurid invasions, which took place in the 11th and 12th centuries.

This is when the language was first introduced to the region. In spite of this, the Mughal era, which began in the 16th century, was the time when Persian reached its pinnacle as the language of the court and the medium of administration.

The Mughal kings being from Central Asia and Turko-Mongol heritage brought with them the cultural and linguistic traditions of Persianate communities. These traditions were passed down from generation to generation. When it came to matters of government, culture, and intellectual pursuits in the Mughal courts, Persian, with its extensive literary tradition, gradually became the language of choice.

There is a syncretism of language:

During the time of the Mughals, the landscape of language was characterized by a syncretic fusion of other languages, including Persian, with indigenous languages. An exceptional linguistic synthesis was produced as a result of the interaction between Persian and the languages spoken in the region, despite the fact that Persian was the language of the court and the elite.

This linguistic syncretism was not confined to the court; rather, it pervaded many different parts of society, including commerce, administration, and cultural interactions. One of the factors that contributed to the development of a linguistic tapestry that reflected the cultural diversity of the Indian subcontinent was the coexistence of Persian with regional languages.

The Persianization of Vocabulary

Incorporation into the Languages of Their Regions:

The incorporation of Persian vocabulary into regional languages was one of the most profound effects that Persian had on the geography of the language world.

Languages such as Urdu, Hindi, Bengali, Punjabi, and others have had their vocabularies enlarged as a result of the significant use of loanwords and idioms from Persian civilization.

The incorporation of Persian linguistic characteristics was observed in the fields of administration, government, literature, commerce, and the arts. The incorporation of Persian language into terms pertaining to government offices, titles, legal concepts, and cultural expressions resulted in the formation of a linguistic fusion that mirrored the cultural synthesis of the Mughal era.

Influence on the Literature of the Vernacular:

Furthermore, Persian's impact spread beyond the realm of courtly language and into the realm of common literature. Poets and scholars writing in regional languages were motivated to embrace and adapt Persian literary forms, meters, and subjects as a result of the Mughal monarchs' encouragement of Persian literature.

Poetic genres such as the ghazal and the masnavi were developed in Urdu and other regional languages as a result of the influence of Persian literary traditions. The vernacular literary traditions that were impacted by Persian poetry were able to find voice for the themes of love, mysticism, and social critique that are abundant in Persian poetry.

The influence of Persian on the languages of the region

Urdu, commonly known as the Persianized vernacular

Origin and Development: Urdu, which is frequently referred to as the "language of the camp" or "Lashkari Zaban," evolved as a unique linguistic heritage during the time of the Mughal dynasty. Languages such as Persian, Turkic, Arabic, and indigenous Indian languages were brought together to form Urdu, which may be traced back to its origins.

The fertile basis for the formation of Urdu was provided by the linguistic milieu that existed within the Mughal courts and contemporary metropolitan areas. The Mughal Empire was known for its pluralistic philosophy, which was reflected in the development of the language as a medium of communication among individuals who came from a variety of linguistic backgrounds.

Structure and Vocabulary: The Persianization of Urdu is especially noticeable in the vocabulary and grammatical structure of the language. The Persian language is the source of a sizable component of the Urdu lexicon, which includes phrases that are associated with aspects of administration, poetry, and cultural expressions. A further manifestation of the impact of Persian calligraphy traditions is the script that is utilized for the writing of Urdu. This script is a derivative of the Persian alphabet that is known as Nasta'līq.

One of the distinguishing features of Urdu is its syntactical structure, which is distinguished from those of other regional languages by its utilization of Persian grammatical forms. Urdu's Persian roots are responsible for a significant portion of its linguistic sophistication, despite the fact that it incorporates many aspects from Arabic and Turkic languages.

Differentiations Across Regions:

It is commonly believed that Urdu is the dominant language that has benefited the most from Persian influence; nonetheless, many regional languages have also undergone linguistic modifications. Regional languages that were spoken in areas where Persian was the predominant language adopted features of Persian to varied degrees.

The incorporation of Persian terminology into Hindi, for instance, may be seen in terms that pertain to governance, culture, and commerce. Devanagari, a script that is derived from Persian and is used for writing Hindi, is another thing that demonstrates the historical linguistic contacts that have taken place between Persian and Hindi.

Legacy of Culture and Literature

Synthesis of Literary Works:

In addition to the vocabulary, the Persian influence on the linguistic environment extended to the literary traditions of the Indian subcontinent. This influence was not limited to vocabulary alone. At the Mughal courts, literary synthesis took place, when Persian literary forms and subjects mixed with regional languages. These courts were hubs of literary synthesis.

Persian literature is responsible for the development of a poetic form known as the ghazal, which eventually became a famous genre in both Persian and regional languages. Urdu poets such as Mirza Ghalib and Allama Iqbal, who were influenced by Persian poetry traditions, produced works that illustrated the language and cultural fusion that was encouraged by the Mughals.

The impact on prose and drama is as follows:

Persian influences were also present in the writing of prose and theatrical literature, in addition to poetry. There is a legacy of storytelling that has been conveyed in both Persian and regional languages. Masnavis, which are narrative poems, are frequently used to express this tradition. The variety of prose and dramatic forms was brought to by the utilization of literary devices, metaphors, and narrative structures that were indigenous to Persian literature.

Particularly influential on the creation of Urdu prose were the narrative techniques that originated in Persian culture. The dastan, which is a type of epic tale, frequently took influence from Persian narratives, which resulted in the creation of a literary tradition that combined different aspects of Persian and local culture.

Titles and Naming Conventions that are Common

The Application of Persian to Names:

In accordance with the cultural standards of the Persianate, the Mughal kings established naming customs and titles that were steeped in the traditions of the Persian religion. In spite of the fact that the personal names of the monarchs frequently indicated their Central Asian and Turkic roots, the titles and honorifics that were bestowed upon them were of a Persian nature.

Connotations that were unique to the Persian language and culture were attached to titles such as "Padishah" (which means "emperor"), "Shahanshah" (which means "king of kings"), and "Jahangir" (which means "conqueror of the world"). A united cultural and linguistic identity was established within the Mughal court through the usage of Persian titles, which were extended to members of the nobility, scholars, poets, and other dignitaries throughout that time.

Adaptations to Certain Regions:

Although titles written in Persian were commonly used, there were regional variations that reflected the language and cultural diversity of the target audience. As a result of the local languages continuing to exert their influence in personal names and titles, a dynamic interaction between Persian and regional linguistic features was created.

A cultural tapestry that embraced the plurality of languages was created as a result of the incorporation of Persian titles with regional naming traditions. This comprehensive approach to names and titles represented the Mughals' aim to promote a sense of cultural unity while yet understanding and appreciating the distinctions that existed between regions.

Recent Perspectives on the Situation

Influence that is still present:

The Persian language continues to have a significant impact on the linguistic landscape of the Indian subcontinent, and this affect lives on in modern times. When it comes to everyday communication, literary expressions, and cultural expressions, the incorporation of Persian terminology into regional languages, particularly Urdu, is something that is readily apparent.

There are a great number of cities, monuments, and cultural traditions all throughout the subcontinent that have names that originally come from the Persian language. You can see the heritage of Persian calligraphy in the official papers, the signage, and the artistic expressions of the Persian people.

The continuing impact that Persian has had on the landscape of language serves as a bridge between the history and the contemporary, which contributes to the complex tapestry of languages that are spoken in the region.

Synthesis of Cultures in Contemporary Perspectives:

The cultural synthesis that was established during the Mughal Empire, which included linguistic contacts between Persian and regional languages, continues to serve as a source of inspiration in modern-day India. The syncretic ethos that was characteristic of the Mughal Empire is celebrated through cultural events, literary works, and idioms that draw from a variety of language traditions.

Elements of Persian culture continue to be highly valued in a variety of professions, including music, calligraphy, and literature. The cultural and linguistic legacy that was left behind by the Mughal Empire serves as a reminder of the interdependence of various linguistic traditions and the ongoing force of cultural synthesis in the process of forming the identity of the Indian subcontinent.

An investigation into the ways in which Persian has influenced the linguistic landscape of the Indian subcontinent has revealed a dynamic interaction between Persian and the languages spoken by individual regions. The Mughal era, which placed a strong focus on cultural synthesis, linguistic diversity, and intellectual contacts, was a significant contributor to the formation of the linguistic traditions that are still in use in modern-day India.

The incorporation of Persian components into naming norms, the Persianization of vocabulary, the emergence of Urdu as a Persianized vernacular, the literary synthesis that took place in both poetry and prose, and the integration of Persian elements into naming customs are all aspects of a rich and complex linguistic tapestry. As a tribute to the historical interconnections that have molded the diverse and heterogeneous character of the Indian subcontinent, the continuing impact of Persian on the linguistic landscape acts as a testament to the interconnections. In spite of the fact that the subcontinent is currently navigating the problems and opportunities of the 21st century, the linguistic influences that were prevalent during the Mughal era continue to contribute to the vibrant tapestry of languages and cultures that are present in the region.

4.3 Introduction of terms like "Hindustan" and their usage during this period

It was during the Mughal era on the Indian subcontinent that not only were there enormous changes in the political and cultural landscape, but there were also substantial developments in the language landscape. During this time period, the introduction and utilization of terminology such as "Hindustan" played a significant influence in the formation of the conceptualization of the region, the formation of its cultural identity, and the interactions between the many linguistic and cultural communities. This investigation investigates the origins and applications of terminology such as "Hindustan" during the Mughal era. It also investigates the historical context of these terms, as well as their linguistic implications and the lasting imprint they have left in current discourse.

In the context of the Mughal era's historical context
The Beginning of the Established Mughal Empire:

In the year 1526, Babur established the Mughal Empire, which marked the beginning of a new chapter in the history of the Indian subcontinent. In addition to their origins in Central Asia, the Mughals carried with them a broad cultural and linguistic background that was able to fit in with the various traditions that were prevalent on the subcontinent. During the time of the Mughals, the political landscape spanned a large and varied territory. In order to effectively administer such a diverse realm, it was necessary to invent and use terminology that could incorporate both the geographical and cultural components of the territory.

Intercultural Communication and the Diversity of Languages:

The Mughal kings, and Akbar in particular, were renowned for their efforts to establish a syncretic culture that was not limited by religious or language constraints. In the Mughal courts, scholars and artists from a variety of cultural and linguistic backgrounds came together to engage in intellectual discourse. These courts developed into thriving hubs of intellectual interaction. This cultural synthesis, in conjunction with the several languages spoken, had an impact on the formation and utilization of terminology that were used to characterize the vast and varied provinces that were under Mughal authority.

The origin and usage of the term "Hindustan"

Etymology and the Origins of the Word:

"Hindustan" is a compound word that originates from the Persian language. It is a combination of the words "Hind," which refers to the Indian subcontinent, and "stan," which means country or area. Since this is the case, the term "Hindustan" might be translated as "Land of the Hindus" or "Land of India."

It is possible to trace its origins back to the medieval Persian and Turkic writings, where it was used to refer to the geographical breadth of the Indian subcontinent where it was first used.

When writing in Persian, historians and chroniclers of the Mughal era frequently used the term "Hindustan" to refer to the areas that were ruled by the Mughals. The memoirs of Babur, known as Baburnama, have a number of occasions in which the phrase is used to describe the territories that he conquered and remained in control over. Over the course of history, the term "Hindustan" came to be synonymous with the Mughal Empire and the cultural fusion that took place within its borders.

Connotations Related to Geography and Social Culture:

Not only did the term "Hindustan" have a geographical sense during the time of the Mughals, but it also had cultural and historical value along with it. It was a word that comprised the various regions that make up the Indian subcontinent, ranging from the Gangetic plains to the Deccan plateau and from the Himalayas to the Indian Ocean. It evolved into a phrase that brought together people and encapsulated the grandeur and diversity of the Mughal Empire for all time.

One further thing that "Hindustan" symbolized was the blending of different cultures and customs that took place throughout the Mughal era. The phrase was broad, reflecting the multicultural attitude of the Mughal Empire, despite the fact that its origin suggested a tie to the regions for whom Hinduism was the predominant religion. Within the wide span of the subcontinent, it accepted the coexistence of a variety of communities that comprised different languages, religious traditions, and cultural traditions.

The implications for linguistics

The Persianization of the Terminology:

The official business of the Mughal courts was done in Persian, which eventually became the language of government, culture, and intellectual conversation. As a result of the Persianization of the Mughal court, the vocabulary that was employed to describe the empire and its provinces underwent a significant transformation. Due to the fact that the word "Hindustan" originates from Persian, it serves as an example of the impact that Persian has had on the global language landscape.

In order to create a linguistic synthesis that was characteristic of the Mughal era, administrative words, geographical designations, and cultural expressions borrowed parts of the Persian language.

It was via the process of Persianizing terminology that the Mughal Empire was able to establish a single linguistic and cultural identity that transcended both linguistic and religious divisions.

Interaction with Languages Spoken in Regional Areas:

The interplay between Persian and regional languages resulted in a linguistic diversity that paralleled the cultural diversity of the Mughal Empire. Persian was the main court language, but regional languages also contributed to the development of Persian. A common linguistic history was established as a result of the incorporation of Persian terminology, which included the term "Hindustan," into their own regional languages.

In areas where Persian was not the primary language spoken, the translation and adaptation of Persian terminology into the languages spoken there indicated a linguistic fusion. "Hindustan" eventually made its way into vernacular languages, with each language modifying it in accordance with the grammatical idiosyncrasies of its own language. This interaction across languages helped to contribute to the establishment of a linguistic tapestry that was not only diverse but also interrelated.

The Importance of Certain Cultural and Historical Factors

The conceptualization of one's identity:

It was during the Mughal era that the term "Hindustan" was used, and it was this usage that had a significant influence in the overall notion of regional and cultural identity. It exemplified a geographical and cultural entity that was not constrained by governmental boundaries or religious connections. In the Mughal Empire, where various linguistic, religious, and cultural communities coexisted and contributed to the complex tapestry of the subcontinent, the term "Hindustan" became a symbol of the synthesis that was taking place within the empire.

The inclusive approach to government that was taken by the Mughal monarchs, as seen by Akbar's policy of Sulh-i-kul (peace with all), was embodied in the word "Hindustan." By recognizing the plurality of the region's people and cultures, it acknowledged the region's pluralism and embraced its diversity.

The Documentation of Historical Events and Their Legacy:

When it came to historical documents, chronicles, and literary works that were published during the Mughal Empire, the term "Hindustan" was utilized quite rather frequently. The phrase was used by the historians of the time to describe the lands that they governed, conquered, or chronicled. These historians wrote their descriptions in Persian.

The historical material that was provided helped to ensure that the phrase would continue to be used in the same manner and that it would leave an enduring legacy in the collective memory of the subcontinent.

In current discourse, the term "Hindustan" is frequently used to refer to the historical and cultural history of the Indian subcontinent. This legacy of "Hindustan" continues to permeate contemporary discourse. A connection is made to the Mughal era and the influence that it had on the cultural and linguistic environment of the region through the use of this monument.

Current usage and interpretations of current terminology

The Geographical and National Identities:

At the present time, the word "Hindustan" is still utilized to refer to the region that is known as the Indian subcontinent. In spite of the fact that the governmental boundaries of the region have changed over time, the name continues to hold significant historical and cultural meaning. The Mughal era and the cultural synthesis that it represented are frequently invoked in lyrical and literary contexts through the use of this phrase, which is frequently employed to generate a sense of nostalgia.

Occasionally, the term "Hindustan" is utilized as an alternate name for the country of India in common usage. However, it is vital to keep in mind that the term contains different implications for different societies, and that its usage might be construed in a variety of different ways. When viewed through the perspective of historical richness and diversity, it may generate a sense of cultural continuity for certain people, while those who view it differently may see it differently.

Unity and Diversity of Cultural Heritage:

In the course of conversations concerning the cultural history that is shared by the Indian subcontinent, the word "Hindustan" is frequently brought up. The concept of a shared past, which is defined by cultural syncretism, linguistic diversity, and historical continuity, is reflected in this theory. Taking this into consideration, the term "Hindustan" becomes a symbol of oneness that is independent of language and theological diversity.

As a result of discussions on the phrase, the necessity of diversity and inclusivity in contemporary discourse has also been brought to light. As a reminder of the significance of creating unity in variety, the historical usage of the term "Hindustan" during the Mughal Empire, which accepted and celebrated diversity, serves as a useful reminder.

During the Mughal era, the introduction and utilization of terminology such as "Hindustan" played a significant role in the conceptualization of the region, the formation of its cultural identity, and the relationships between many communities that were linguistically and culturally diverse. The word, which had its origins in Persian but was copied and adopted by people of many languages, encapsulated the expanse and diversity of the Mughal Empire beyond international borders.

The name "Hindustan" was more than just a geographical location; it was also a symbol of the cultural synthesis, plurality, and inclusiveness that were hallmarks of the Mughal era. It is the historical legacy of the phrase that continues to endure in current discourse, where it continues to convey a sense of shared heritage and togetherness among the people of the Indian subcontinent. As the region navigates the complexities of the 21st century, the historical usage of the term "Hindustan" continues to serve as a poignant reminder of the interconnection of linguistic, cultural, and historical narratives in the process of forming the identity of the subcontinent.

Chapter 5

Colonial Encounters and Naming Politics

During the time of colonial authority on the Indian subcontinent, many facets of the country's sociopolitical and cultural landscape saw significant transformations. These transformations were brought about by the entry of European powers and their subsequent rule over the region. The reorganization of names, both geographical and personal, was a crucial aspect of this shift. It reflected the imposition of colonial power and the altering of identities throughout the process. This investigation digs into the colonial encounters and naming politics that took place in the Indian subcontinent. It investigates the influence that European colonization had on toponyms and anthroponyms, as well as the broader implications for cultural, social, and political identity.

The First European Contacts and the Naming Practices of the People
Portuguese and Early Maritime Contacts: Relationships and

It is possible to trace the origins of the first meetings with European powers in the Indian subcontinent back to the Portuguese travels that took place in the latter half of the Renaissance. Maritime contacts were established with the coastal regions of India by Portuguese navigators who were looking for new trade routes. In the course of their commercial activities and the establishment of colonies, they frequently gave new names to locations based on their linguistic preferences or the cultural connotations they had with those locations.

This marked the beginning of a pattern that would be continued and built upon by successive colonial powers. The application of European names to already existing communities and geographical features signified the beginning of this trend. These earliest practices of name laid the groundwork for the more extensive naming politics that would develop over the course of the centuries that European colonialism would affect.

Influence from the Dutch and the Danes:

They followed in the footsteps of the Portuguese and established commercial posts and colonies in various parts of the Indian subcontinent. The Dutch and the Danish were also involved. The rearrangement of names was further influenced by their interactions with the indigenous communities as well as the introduction of European settlements.

For example, the Dutch renamed the city of Madras to Fort St. George, which reflected the East India Company's military and commercial interests in the region. In a similar manner, the names that were given to Danish villages and forts reflected the aims and perspectives of European governments. An impression was left on the toponymic landscape as a result of these early cases of renaming, which were frequently motivated by the desire to assert colonial power.

The Colonialism of the British Empire and the Politics of Naming

The East India Company and the Changes in Administrative Structure:

The arrival of the British East India Company in the 17th century was a watershed moment in the history of colonial interactions in the Indian subcontinent. This event marked the beginning of the West India Company. Over the course of the progressive consolidation of British authority, the East India Company came to take administrative control over large regions. The naming practices and the politics of identity were profoundly affected by this change in governance, which had major ramifications.

The British, in their capacity as administrators, initiated the process of renaming cities, towns, and administrative entities in order to better accommodate their administrative needs. An illustration of this would be the metamorphosis of the existing village of Kalikata into the city of Calcutta. Not only did this process of renaming reflect linguistic preferences, but it also signified the imposition of colonial power on the toponymic environment where it was carried out.

The Inversion of Place Names into English:

The Anglicization of place names became a common practice as British rule expanded over the region throughout time. In order to make the native names more understandable to the colonial administration and settlers, the British attempted to replace them with anglicized versions of the names. This process of renaming frequently includes the transcription or modification of native names in order to bring them into better alignment with the phonetics of the English language.

Take, for example, the city of Bombay, which was originally known as "Bom Bahia" but later changed its name to "Bombay" due to the influence of the Portuguese language. Not only was this language change a sign of the cultural and political supremacy of the British colonial power, but it was also a manifestation of the Anglicization of place names.

Networks of Railways and Telegraphs:

It was during the time of British colonial rule that the construction of transportation and communication infrastructure, such as the railway and telegraph networks, played a significant part in the process of renaming locations.

As these networks evolved, British officials frequently forced new names on railway stations, cities, and landmarks. These names reflected not just the effect of colonial power but also the influence of technological improvements on naming conventions.

The process of standardizing names for the purpose of making communication and administration more straightforward resulted in the imposition of English names on locations that in the past may have been designated by a variety of languages. The dominance of English as the language of power and administration was strengthened as a result of this trend, which resulted in the marginalization of all local languages and identities.

Relevance to Linguistics and Culture
Indigenous peoples' identities are being suppressed:
Indigenous peoples' identities and languages were profoundly impacted by the naming practices that were prevalent throughout colonial times. There was a contribution to the repression of local identities and cultural heritage that was made by the renaming of sites, which frequently involved the erasure or marginalization of indigenous names. The imposition of anglicized names resulted in the reinforcement of a hierarchical linguistic order, in which English was raised to a higher level than native languages.

There were several instances in which the act of renaming led to the loss of historical and cultural ties that were traditionally associated with indigenous names. Not only did the removal of pre-colonial toponyms indicate a shift in language, but it also showed an intentional endeavor to alter and control the historical narrative of the region.

The Influence on the Recollection of Culture:
It is also important to note that the renaming of locations throughout the colonial period had a long-lasting effect on cultural memory. Local communities experienced a sense of cultural dislocation as a result of the elimination of indigenous names, which contributed to the alteration of toponyms, which became symbols of colonial imposition. There was a disruption in the continuity of cultural memory as a result of the loss of familiar place names, which also contributed to a feeling of alienation from geographical surroundings.

A further deterioration of the connection between the local community and their cultural legacy was brought about by the renaming of historical locations, religious places, and natural monuments. The cultural and historical value that was encoded in indigenous names was frequently neglected or discarded by the British colonial authorities, who placed a higher priority on the imposition of names that mirrored European ideas.

Classifications Based on Anthropological and Ethnographic Knowledge
The Census and the Classification of Ethnographic Groups:
During the time of colonial rule, anthropological and ethnographic categories, which were crucial in the process of naming practices, were institutionalized during this time period. Because of the necessity for administrative control and categorization, the British colonial authorities engaged in the systematic classification of ethnic groupings, castes, and tribes. This exercise was driven by the requirement for administrative control.

The purpose of the census operations that were carried out by the British was to develop complete classifications of the various populations that were already present on the subcontinent. In many cases, these classifications were based on linguistic, religious, and caste affiliations. These classifications contributed to the formation of identity categories, which were subsequently reflected in official papers and administrative records.

The process of standardizing names:

The categorization of communities and the standardization of names in official documents has repercussions for the identities of both individuals and groups. By providing standardized names for administrative convenience, colonial administrations frequently grouped individuals and communities according to linguistic and religious factors. This was done in order to facilitate information management.

Although this kind of standardization helped to streamline administrative operations, it frequently resulted in an oversimplification of complex social structures and historical identities. Names were given to individuals and communities, and it is possible that these names did not accurately reflect their self-identified or regionally recognized identities.

The Post-Colonial Era and the Persistence of Naming Politics

Initiatives pertaining to independence and renaming:

During the middle of the 20th century, British colonial rule in the Indian subcontinent came to an end, which ultimately resulted in the foundation of sovereign nations. Reclaiming indigenous names and undoing the linguistic and cultural impositions that had been imposed during the colonial period were both activities that were undertaken in the aftermath of independence.

The country of India, for instance, has implemented a number of renaming projects, which have resulted in the return of numerous anglicized place names to their pre-colonial designations. The names of cities such as Mumbai (which was originally Bombay), Kolkata (which was formerly Calcutta), and Chennai (which was formerly Madras) were changed in an effort to represent the linguistic and cultural authenticity of the cities.

Challenges and a Legacy That Are Still Present:

Despite the fact that post-colonial efforts have been made to reclaim indigenous names, the legacy of colonial naming practices continues to persist over time. There are numerous cities, landmarks, and organizations that continue to use the anglicized names that were given to them throughout the historical period of colonialism. The fact that these names have persisted over time is evidence of the persistent impact that colonial history has had on toponymy and cultural memory in the modern generation.

There are other difficulties that develop while attempting to navigate the complexities of multiple cultural and linguistic identities that exist within post-colonial societies. There are many different linguistic communities that are looking for representation and acknowledgment, and the naming of locations, streets, and organizations can be a sensitive matter. In post-colonial naming politics, one of the major challenges is to find a way to strike a balance between the imperative of national unity and the need for linguistic diversity.

Colonial contacts in the Indian subcontinent, which were characterized by European powers imposing their linguistic and cultural viewpoints on the toponymic environment, had far-reaching effects for identities, memories, and cultural legacy. These encounters left a lasting impression on the Indian subcontinent. The colonial enterprise had a number of essential components, including the renaming of locations, the standardization of names, and classifications based on linguistic and ethnographic factors.

The post-colonial toponymic landscape and the issues that newly independent nations face were both shaped by the linguistic and cultural implications of colonial naming practices, which continued beyond the era of period in which colonial name practices were in effect. Despite the fact that ongoing efforts have been made to reclaim indigenous names and demonstrate linguistic authenticity, the legacy of colonial naming politics continues to be a complicated and nuanced feature of the history of the region.

The investigation of name politics offers vital insights into the diverse nature of post-colonial issues at a time when the Indian subcontinent is struggling to come to terms with the historical imprint of colonial encounters on its linguistic and cultural identities. It highlights how important it is to acknowledge the various linguistic and cultural histories that exist while simultaneously negotiating the complications of national unity and identity in the modern period.

5.1 Analysis of how the British colonial period influenced naming conventions

The time of British colonial rule in the Indian subcontinent, which lasted from the 17th century to the middle of the 20th century, had a significant influence on a variety of aspects of the region's sociocultural, political, and linguistic landscape. One of the most prominent aspects of this effect was the alteration of naming practices, which included both toponyms (names of places) and anthroponyms (names of people). The purpose of this research is to investigate the ways in which the British colonial period influenced name practices on the Indian subcontinent. Specifically, the analysis will investigate the reasons behind renaming, the language changes that occurred, the cultural implications, and the legacy that continues to bear on contemporary nomenclature.

The Reasons Behind the Renaming of Items

Convenience in Administrative Matters:

Administrative convenience was one of the key reasons that locations were renamed during the time when the British colonial government was in power. The requirement for effective administration became of the utmost importance as the East India Company expanded its grip over previously uncontrolled territory. Those administrators who spoke English but were not familiar with the linguistic complexities of the subcontinent faced difficulties when dealing with the existing indigenous names, which were frequently varied and had their origins in the local languages.

Anglicized forms of place names were introduced by the British in order to facilitate the streamlining of governance and communication. As a result of the process of Anglicization, these names became more accessible to colonial authorities and settlers, which made it easier for administrative machinery to work. For the purpose of maximizing administrative effectiveness, this incentive for renaming mirrored the imposition of colonial power on the toponymic environment.

An assertion of cultural and ideological beliefs:

Additionally, the British colonial authorities used the practice of renaming locations as a means of asserting their cultural and ideological beliefs. They were able to demonstrate their authority and control over the lands that they commanded through this tangible expression. The process of renaming frequently involved the deletion or marginalization of native names, which served to reinforce the narrative of British superiority and the imposition of European cultural norms.

When towns, landmarks, and geographical features were renamed in the image of British principles, it led to a sense of cultural hegemony in the people of the United Kingdom.

As a result of the adoption of names that mirrored British historical figures, monarchy, or geographical phrases, the colonial narrative was strengthened, and a Eurocentric worldview was projected onto the toponymic environment.

Changes in the Languages Used

Anglicization of toponyms, which includes:

The toponyms of the Indian subcontinent underwent a considerable linguistic alteration during the time that the British colonial government was in control of the region. In order to make native names more appealing to people who know English, the process of Anglicizing place names involves changing the names of the places. This process frequently resulted in the toponyms that were already in use being simplified, distorted, or ultimately replaced entirely.

As an illustration, the city of Calicut was renamed Calcutta, Madras was turned into Chennai, and Bombay was transformed into Mumbai. Not only did these alterations reflect linguistic preferences, but they also contributed to the erasure of the linguistic and cultural diversity that was encoded in the names that were originally used. Through the process of Anglicization, the dominance of English as the language of power and administration was strengthened, which resulted in the marginalization of individual languages and identities.

Homogenization and Standardization of the Process:

Creating a toponymic landscape that was consistent across the board was the goal of the British colonial rulers, who sought to standardize and homogenize place names. Standardization entailed establishing a single name for a location, which was frequently transformed into an anglicized form, regardless of the linguistic and cultural variety of the area. The goal to streamline both administration and communication was the impetus behind this manner of doing things.

The process of standardization often resulted in the loss of linguistic nuances and historical meanings that were embedded in indigenous names. In favor of a standardized toponymic system that mirrored the language preferences of the colonial rulers, local variances and linguistic diversity were sacrificed. This was done in order to achieve the stated goal.

Implications for Culture

The suppression of indigenous peoples' identities:

During the time of British colonial rule, the renaming of locations had significant cultural repercussions, which contributed to the disappearance of indigenous identities. It was common for indigenous names to carry cultural, religious, or historical importance because they were strongly rooted in the languages and histories of the local community. It was an attempt to replace these rich and diverse cultural ties with names that were more in line with British ideas, and the imposition of anglicized names signified this attempt.

This erasing of indigenous identities went beyond language alterations; it was something that was done on purpose in order to rewrite the cultural story of the region. The toponyms that were anglicized became symbols of colonial dominance, which resulted in the displacement of the pre-colonial cultural memory that was embedded in indigenous names.

The Imposition of Cultural Regulations from Europe:

It was also a reflection of the imposition of European cultural norms and values on the Indian subcontinent that the renaming of geographical locations occurred. It was common practice to draw inspiration for the new names from historical individuals, buildings, and geographical phrases that were associated with Europe. Not only did this technique contribute to the marginalization of local cultural references, but it also served to cement the Eurocentric perspective.

In spite of the fact that the subcontinent possesses a wide cultural and historical legacy, the introduction of names such as Victoria, Albert, or King's Cross gave the impression that there was a cultural continuity with the territory of the British Isles. A colonial mindset that aimed to transform the cultural landscape in the image of the colonizers was reflected in this action.

An Enduring Legacy in the Development of Modern Nomenclature

Initiatives for Post-Colonial Renaming are as follows:

Post-colonial initiatives to reclaim indigenous names and demonstrate linguistic authenticity began with the end of the British colonial period, which marked the beginning of these efforts. Following their attainment of independence, a number of nations located on the Indian subcontinent launched renaming efforts with the purpose of reclaiming their cultural identities and reconstructing their pre-colonial toponyms.

As a result of these attempts, cities such as Kolkata (which was once known as Calcutta), Mumbai (which was formerly known as Bombay), and Chennai (which was formerly known as Madras) received name changes. As a result of these efforts, the linguistic and cultural impositions that were imposed during the colonial period were intended to be undone, and the significance of indigenous names in expressing the diversity of the region was reaffirmed.

The Persistence of Historic Colonial Legacies:

Furthermore, the legacy of British colonial name practices continues to be present in contemporary nomenclature, despite the fact that post-colonial renaming attempts have been implemented. There are numerous cities, landmarks, and organizations that continue to use the anglicized names that were given to them throughout the historical period of colonialism. The fact that these names have persisted until the present day is evidence of the persistent impact that colonial history has had on the toponymic landscape and the cultural memory.

On top of that, the Anglicization of personal names, particularly surnames, is still widely practiced in certain groups. Families that obtained anglicized surnames during the time of colonial rule frequently continue to use them now, which contributes to the survival of colonial legacies in personal nomenclature.

Difficulties and Complicated Situations

Keeping the Diversity of Linguistics in Check:

When it comes to renaming projects in the post-colonial period, there are issues involved in striking a balance between the imperative of national unity and the plurality of languages. There are a great number of languages and dialects spoken on the Indian subcontinent, each of which has its own distinct toponymic traditions. It is necessary to handle the complications of linguistic variety within the context of efforts to standardize names or reclaim indigenous names in order to guarantee representation and inclusivity.

The Art of Handling Historical Complicatedness:

When renaming locations in the post-colonial age, it is necessary to navigate the complexity of history and to acknowledge the layers of significance that are inscribed in both colonial and indigenous names. A sensitive process that involves careful consideration of a variety of perspectives and sensitivities is the act of striking a balance between honoring historical continuity and recovering cultural authenticity.

During the time when the British colonial government was in control of the Indian subcontinent, naming traditions were irrevocably altered. Toponyms and anthroponyms were reshaped to represent the objectives and values of the colonial government. The erasure of indigenous identities and the imposition of European cultural norms were both contributed to by the objectives behind renaming, which were driven by administrative convenience, cultural assertion, and linguistic alteration.

The lingering legacy of colonial naming standards continues to be present in contemporary nomenclature, despite the fact that post-colonial organizations have attempted to restore indigenous names and demonstrate linguistic authenticity. Within the context of the post-colonial era, arguments concerning names continue to be shaped by the difficulties of balancing linguistic diversity, resolving historical complexity, and addressing the complexities of identity.

Providing insights into the multidimensional nature of linguistic and cultural transitions in the Indian subcontinent, the research of how the British colonial period influenced naming conventions contributes to the understanding of these transformations. The fact that names continue to be significant in representing historical narratives, cultural identities, and the intricate relationship between colonial legacies and post-colonial aspirations is brought to light by this.

5.2 Introduction of terms like "East India Company" and their implications

The phrase "East India Company" conjures up a period in the history of global trade, colonization, and the establishment of empires that is intricate and diverse. In particular, the introduction of such terminology during the period of European expansion and mercantilism in the Indian subcontinent had far-reaching ramifications that impacted the socio-economic, political, and cultural landscapes. These effects were particularly significant in the Indian subcontinent. This investigation goes into the origins of phrases such as "East India Company" and the implications that they carry. It investigates the historical backdrop, the role that the Company played, and the lasting impact that it had on the regions that it interacted with.

Contextualization of the Past

At the same time, European trading companies began to emerge

The 16th and 17th centuries saw the establishment of European trading corporations that were looking for new routes to Asia, with a particular focus on the Indian subcontinent. A substantial number of European countries established trading endeavors in faraway lands for a variety of reasons, including the demand for luxury items, the spice trade, and the possibility of rich business.

A maritime empire that comprised trading posts in India was established by the Portuguese, who were among the first people to explore into the Indian Ocean. It wasn't long before other European powers, such as the Dutch and the English, followed suit. Significant milestones in the institutionalization of European trade and colonial ambitions were marked by the establishment of the Dutch East India Company (VOC) in 1602 and the English East India Company (EIC) in 1600. Both of these companies were established before the year 1600.

The English East India Company:

A monopoly on English trade with the East Indies was handed to the English East India Company, which had been licensed by Queen Elizabeth I on the occasion of her reign. The establishment of this corporation signified the beginning of a corporate entity that would go on to play a significant part in determining the course of events for the Indian subcontinent. The mandate of the Company comprised the establishment of economic contacts, the acquisition of territory, and the participation in diplomatic and military activities for the purpose of protecting its interests.

It was the founding of the English East India Company that laid the groundwork for a new chapter in the history of global commerce. This new phase was defined by the appearance of joint-stock firms that were granted significant powers by royal charters. The effects of such corporate bodies on commerce, diplomacy, and colonialism were significant and would continue to resonate for generations to come following their establishment.

The East India Company's Functions and Activities in the Indian Ocean
Trade and commercial activity:

The major objective of the East India Company was to engage in commercial transactions with the East Indies, with a special focus on the Indian subcontinent and Southeast Asia. The Company's objective was to establish a monopoly on the lucrative spice trade as well as the interchange of other goods including textiles, indigo, saltpeter, and opium. The Company's policies and actions were predominantly influenced by the desire of profit, which served as a driving factor.

Manufacturing facilities and trading posts were established along the coast of India as part of the Company's commercial operations. The European merchants who traded with the indigenous merchants and intermediaries interacted with one another at these sites, which functioned as hubs for the exchange of products. With the goal of securing important resources and establishing a dominant position in the Indian Ocean trade network, the Company's influence spread to a number of different places, ranging from the Coromandel Coast to Bengal and beyond.

Expansion of Territorial Boundaries:

The role of the East India Company extended beyond the realm of commerce, and it gradually began to develop into a territorial power. These strategic concerns, which included the goal to secure a stable environment for trade and to counter the influence of rival European powers, were the driving force behind the purchase of lands in India.

The military capabilities of the Company were utilized in fights with local forces, and the Company's triumphs in engagements such as Plassey (1757) and Buxar (1764) brought about a considerable expansion of its territorial holdings. The formation of the dual administration system, in which officials of the Company worked in conjunction with local rulers or maintained indirect authority over regions, became a defining characteristic of the Company's colonial rule.

Administration and Diplomacy:

As the East India Company's sphere of influence grew, it took on the responsibility of governance in the areas that it governed. The Company built a system of administration, which included the nomination of Company officials as administrators and the construction of administrative structures to administer revenue, justice, and local affairs. This system was formed by the Company.

The interactions that the Company had with the local authorities, as well as the development of treaties and alliances, were absolutely essential components of the Company's diplomatic activities. Because it was both a trader and an administrator, it was necessary to engage in diplomatic activities in order to successfully negotiate the complexities of the local political system and protect its commercial interests.

Implications of the East India Company
Modifications to the Economic System:

The presence of the East India Company had significant repercussions on the economic landscape of the geographical region known as the Indian subcontinent. The Company's monopoly on some commodities and its control over trade routes were two factors that led to the fundamental changes that occurred in the economies of both Europe and Asia. Restructuring of global economic systems was brought about by the movement of products, capital, and resources between the East and the West.

The role that the Company had in the introduction of new varieties of crops and industries, such as the cultivation of indigo and the manufacturing of silk, had a long-lasting impact on the agricultural economy of regions that were under its influence.

Some people experienced economic prosperity as a result of the change of traditional economies to meet the demands of Europeans, while others were exploited and impoverished as a result of this shift.

Their Influence on Society and Culture:

The East India Company had a significant cultural impact on the Indian subcontinent, which manifested itself in a variety of ways. European, Indian, and Southeast Asian influences came together in the trading posts and communities that were established by the Company. These places became cultural crossroads. The exchange of cultural ideas took place in a variety of domains, including the arts, architecture, food, and language.

The dissemination of Christianity and the introduction of European education, both of which are frequently connected with the activities of the Company, had a long-lasting impact on the civilizations that were present at the time. Missionary work, the establishment of schools, and the founding of colleges all became channels through which Western ideas and ideals were transferred to other parts of the world.

Consequences for the Political System:

The actions of the East India Company had significant political repercussions, which in turn influenced the pattern of events that occurred throughout the history of India. The territorial expansion of the Company, which was motivated by commercial and strategic factors, resulted in the development of a de facto colonial rule over broad territory.

The dual administration system followed by the Company, in which native rulers worked together with officials from the Company, had repercussions for the political systems of indigenous communities. Tensions were developed as a result of the dismantling of conventional power institutions and the development of indirect colonial control, which provided the framework for subsequent political shifts.

Colonialism's Founding Principles:

It is common practice to refer to the East India Company as a trade organization; yet, it was the East India Company that was instrumental in establishing the groundwork for formal colonialism on the Indian subcontinent. The transformation from a commercial business to a colonial power was distinguished by the purchase of territories, the establishment of administrative institutions, and the increasing influence over the activities of the local community.

The operations of the Company established precedents for succeeding colonial administrations, as other European powers observed and imitated the Company's techniques because of its success. The transition of the East India Company from a commercial company to a territorial power served as a precursor to the subsequent period of direct colonial control that would take place.

The Legacy and Its Relevance in the Present Day
A Legacy That Will Last:
The East India Company left behind a legacy that continues to be reflected in the historical, economic, and cultural narratives of the Indian subcontinent and beyond. The Company was responsible for initiating economic developments, which provided the framework for the incorporation of the Indian subcontinent into the global capitalist system. The social and cultural exchanges that took place between the East and the West during the time of the Company continue to have an impact on the identities and expressions of culture that are prevalent in the modern day.

During the middle of the 19th century, the British Crown began the process of formally colonizing India. The political ramifications of the Company's operations laid the groundwork for this process. Following the Company's territory conquests and the establishment of administrative structures, the basis for eventual colonial control was built.

On the other hand, historical debates:
There are some contentious issues surrounding the legacy left by the East India Company. Critiques have been leveled against it for numerous reasons, including its role in economic exploitation, the imposition of unequal treaties, and the influence it has had on local industry. In addition to adding another layer of complexity to its historical legacy, the Company's role in the opium trade, which had disastrous implications in China, is also a significant factor.

It is common practice to include talks about the conduct and repercussions of the East India Company in debates concerning reparations, restitution, and historical accountability. Discussions regarding the duties of companies and the lasting influence of colonial legacies continues to be prompted by the historical role of the Company, which continues to be a subject of research and reflection.

Governance and accountability of corporations:
The organizational structure of the East India Company, which includes a joint-stock form and the ability to make decisions independently, provides insights into the development of corporate governance. As a result of the activities of the Company, questions were raised regarding the appropriate balance between economic objectives and ethical considerations. This is a topic that continues to be relevant in contemporary conversations about the accountability of corporations.

The experiences that were gained during the time of the East India Company contribute to ongoing conversations about the roles that businesses play in international politics, the importance of ethical business practices, and the influence that economic operations have on the communities that they are located in.

The period of time in world history that was distinguished by the introduction of names such as "East India Company" when Europe was expanding its territory was a moment of profound change. The actions of the Company had far-reaching and diverse repercussions, which influenced the political, cultural, and economic landscapes of the Indian subcontinent and beyond. As it progressed from its beginnings as a commercial enterprise to its transformation into a territorial power, the East India Company was an essential factor in the development of colonialism and the altering of international relations on a worldwide scale.

Reflections on the complexities of historical interactions, the repercussions of economic and political power, and the responsibilities of businesses in molding the fates of nations are opportunities that are afforded by the continuing legacy of the East India Company. In spite of the fact that the world is still struggling to come to terms with the repercussions of global business and the legacies of colonialism, the historical lessons that should be learned from the time of the East India Company continue to be relevant in terms of comprehending the dynamics of our linked world.

5.3 Examination of colonial maps and the standardization of geographical names

During the time period of European colonialism, maps of the colonies were extremely important in terms of changing how people perceived, understood, and governed the lands that they visited. The act of mapping not only served as a tool for demonstrating colonial authority, economic exploitation, and cultural supremacy, but it also represented the geographical knowledge that was prevalent throughout that time period. The standardization of geographical names was an important component of this mapping endeavor that was undertaken. This investigation goes into the procedures of colonial mapping and the standardization of geographical names. It investigates the reasons behind these practices, the impact they had on indigenous identities, and the legacy that they left behind in post-colonial toponymy.

Cartography and the Aspirations of Colonialism
The Powerful Role of Mapping in History:

The expansionist aspirations of European nations throughout the period of discovery and colonization were inextricably related to the practice of colonial mapping. For the purpose of providing a visual representation of territorial claims, trading routes, and resources, maps were utilized. Not only were they portrayals of landscapes that were objective, but they were also instruments of power that served to support and legitimize the authority of colonial governments.

Colonial cartographers, who frequently worked under the auspices of imperial powers, played an essential part in the process of converting the intricate and varied landscapes of newly discovered regions into standardized maps. Not only were these maps designed to aid in navigating, but they also served as devices for managing, organizing, and exploiting the territories that were under colonial rule.

Reasons for the Practice of Mapping:

When mapping was done during the time of colonial rule, there were many different and complex reasons for doing so. Through the process of mapping newly found regions, claiming possession of those territories, and delineating boundaries, European nations attempted to assert their dominance. In addition, economic factors played a role in the process of mapping. These included the identification of important resources, trade routes, and potential locations for colonization.

Combined with imperial competition, scientific curiosity served as an additional driving force behind the mapping effort. For the sake of enhancing their geopolitical, economic, and strategic interests, European countries made investments in scientific expeditions, surveys, and mapmaking. These endeavors were undertaken with the intention of exploring and comprehending the world.

The Convention on the Standardization of Geographical Names
Obstacles Concerning Language:

Colonial cartographers had a number of difficulties, one of which was the linguistic diversity of the regions that they were attempting to locate and map. An intricate linguistic environment was presented as a result of the multitude of indigenous languages, dialects, and toponymic traditions that were present. As a result of their lack of familiarity with the local languages, European mapmakers frequently encountered challenges while attempting to authentically portray indigenous names.

In order to overcome these linguistic obstacles and to make communication between colonial officials and settlers easier, there was a desire to standardize geographical names in accordance with the standards of European language. This process entailed transliteration, anglicization, or simplification of native names, which ultimately resulted in the construction of a toponymic landscape that mirrored the preferences of Europeans in terms of language.

The Imposition of Perspectives from Colonialism:

The process of standardizing geographical names was not just an exercise in language, but it was also a representation of the colonial viewpoints that were imposed on the toponymic environment. When European nations were attempting to exert control over newly acquired territories, they imprinted their own cultural and historical references on the maps.

It was common practice to substitute indigenous names that were significant in terms of culture, history, or religion with names that were derived from European kings, colonial administrators, or historical people. This process of renaming not only helped to the eradication of indigenous identities and cultural allusions, but it also simplified the toponymic environment for Europeans when it came to interpreting it.

The Effects on the Identities of Indigenous Peoples
The Erasure of Culture:

The process of standardizing geographical names had a significant influence on the identities of indigenous peoples and the cultural landscapes they inhabited. Native American toponyms that held profound cultural, historical, and spiritual importance were frequently obliterated as a consequence of the imposition of European names.

This cultural erasure went beyond linguistic alterations and included the eradication of local tales that were encoded in place names.

In many cases, the different cultural histories that are associated with monuments, rivers, mountains, and cities were overlooked when they were renamed. With the replacement of their traditional names with European toponyms, indigenous tribes, whose identities were inextricably linked to the land, were confronted with the prospect of losing their cultural continuity.

A Decrease in Knowledge of Geography:

A further factor that contributed to the loss of spatial knowledge among indigenous populations was the standardization of geographical nomenclature. The traditional toponyms of a region frequently contained important information about the topography, ecology, and resources of the area. During the process of European names replacing indigenous ones, the precise spatial knowledge that was inscribed in local toponyms was either ignored or lost.

The indigenous people experienced a loss of spatial knowledge, which had practical ramifications for them. This loss affected their capacity to move, manage resources, and preserve cultural traditions that were related to particular geographies. The removal of indigenous names and their replacement with European ones represented a more widespread rupture in the relationship that existed between indigenous peoples and the areas that they had inhabited for generations.

In the realm of post-colonial toponymy, the enduring legacy
Initiatives for Post-Colonial Renaming are as follows:

In post-colonial toponymy, the legacy of colonial mapping activities and the standardization of geographical names continues to be present. Following the attainment of their independence, a number of countries that had previously been colonies began renaming their countries in order to recover their indigenous names and demonstrate their cultural uniqueness.

Changes were made to cities, landmarks, and geographical features in order to restore to pre-colonial toponyms or adopt names that reflected the languages spoken in the area and the cultural histories of the indigenous people. A sense of pride and a connection to the land were intended to be restored through the implementation of these measures, which tried to correct the historical impositions of colonial names.

Colonial Legacies That Are Still Present:

Even though there have been efforts made to rename areas after colonial rule, the lasting effects of colonial toponymy are still visible in numerous localities. The persistence of European names in current nomenclature is a reflection of the fact that European names continue to be used in locations such as maps, cities, and institutions. The continued use of these names frequently becomes a contentious issue, which in turn sparks conversations about historical memory, identity, and the ongoing influence of colonial legacies.

In certain instances, post-colonial nations struggle with the difficulty of striking a balance between the necessity of linguistic diversity and cultural authenticity and the practical considerations of communication and administration. An feature of post-colonial toponymic landscapes that continues to be a problematic one is the tension that exists between the preservation of indigenous toponyms and the acknowledgment of the historical imprint of colonial names.

Obstacles and Things to Take Into Account

Keeping the Diversity of Linguistics in Check:

In post-colonial toponymy, one of the ongoing issues is striking a balance between the linguistic diversity that exists and the necessity of meeting the practical necessities of communication and administration. Numerous post-colonial states are distinguished by the presence of a plethora of languages and dialects, each of which has its own distinctive toponymic historical practices. It is necessary to handle the complications of linguistic variety within the context of efforts to standardize names or reclaim indigenous names in order to guarantee representation and inclusivity.

Recognizing the Complicated Nature of the Heritage:

Recognizing the historical complexities that are ingrained in both colonial and indigenous names is a necessary step in the process of renaming locations in post-colonial circumstances. The process of striking a balance between conserving historical continuity and regaining cultural authenticity is a complex one that involves careful consideration of a variety of perspectives and sensitivity levels.

The delicate relationship that exists between cartography, colonial goals, and the imposition of European viewpoints on the toponymic environment is shown through the investigation of colonial maps and the standardization of geographical names. Because of linguistic difficulties and colonial reasons, the standardization of names had far-reaching ramifications for indigenous identities, cultural landscapes, and spatial knowledge. These implications were pushed by the name standardization.

It is important to note that the persistent legacy of colonial toponymy in post-colonial settings highlights the continuous impact that historical impositions have on modern identities. The delicate relationship that exists between names, power, and cultural memory is reflected in the difficulties that post-colonial states encounter when attempting to strike a balance between the cultural diversity of their languages, acknowledge the complexities of their histories, and address the complexities of their identities. In a time when the globe is still struggling to come to terms with the legacies of colonialism, the examination of colonial maps and toponymic standardization provides useful insights into the complexity of traversing past narratives and asserting cultural identity in the present.

Chapter 6

The Struggle for Independence and Identity

There is a recurrent theme in the history of nations that is the struggle for independence. This struggle is characterized by movements, revolutions, and struggles to break free from colonial or tyrannical domination. As communities and nations struggle with issues pertaining to self-determination, cultural autonomy, and the building of a collective sense of self, this narrative is intricately connected with the search for identity. An examination of historical instances, the role of leaders and movements, the impact on cultural identities, and the ongoing issues in the post-independence era are all topics that are covered in this investigation, which digs into the varied aspects of the struggle for independence and identity.

Contextualization of the Past

The struggle for independence and the legacy of colonialism:

The struggle for independence frequently takes place within the framework of colonial rule, which is characterized by the assertion of control over territory, resources, and inhabitants by foreign powers. The history of colonization is characterized by the enslavement of indigenous peoples economically, the hegemonic control of culture, and the exploitation of indigenous peoples. Resistance movements began to take shape as colonial powers established their domination over the native population. These movements were motivated by a desire for autonomy and the regaining of cultural identities.

Movements for independence were sparked by the emergence of colonial empires in Africa, Asia, and the Americas. These movements were fueled by the desire of indigenous populations to break free from the shackles of foreign domination. These groups were brought together by a shared desire for self-governance and the protection of cultural differences. This desire was expressed through military resistance, diplomatic talks, or cultural revival.

Impact of World Wars on the World:

Both of the world wars that occurred in the 20th century had a significant impact on the fight for independence. The aftermath of World War I was marked by the dissolution of empires and the redrawing of borders, which provided opportunities for nationalist movements to stake their claim to power.

The concept of national self-determination rose to prominence in the discourse that emerged in the aftermath of the conflict, serving as a framework that enabled independence movements to achieve legitimacy.

Further acceleration of the decolonization process was brought about by World War II. During the war, colonies were motivated to fight for their conquerors, which brought to light the inconsistencies that were inherent in colonialism. A wave of decolonization that swept over Asia, Africa, and the Middle East was made possible by the geopolitical landscape that emerged after the war. This landscape was influenced by the advent of superpowers and the changing dynamics of the global environment.

Movements and Their Leaders

Mahatma Gandhi and the Nonviolent Struggle in India:

The peaceful resistance and civil disobedience that Mahatma Gandhi preached for had a significant impact on the war for independence in India. He was a leader who campaigned for these strategies. In order to resist British control, the Indian National Congress, which was led by Gandhi, devised a strategy that included non-cooperation, boycotts, and peaceful protests. There were two significant events that occurred during India's struggle for independence: the Salt March in 1930 and the Quit India Movement in 1942.

Satyagraha, also known as truth-force, was Gandhi's ideology that highlighted the transformative power of nonviolence in the context of fighting repressive regimes throughout his lifetime. His method not only played a role in India's eventual independence in 1947, but it also left an indelible mark on movements all over the world that advocated for civil rights and social justice after his death.

On the other hand, Nelson Mandela and the fight against apartheid:

It was a long and difficult fight for racial equality and democratic rights in South Africa, and the struggle against apartheid was a struggle that lasted for a long time. While leading the African National Congress (ANC) in a fight against the discriminatory practices of the apartheid state, Nelson Mandela emerged as a key figure in this movement. He was a leader of the African National Congress.

Mandela's release in 1990 represented a significant turning moment in South Africa's history. His imprisonment for 27 years became a symbol of resistance, and his liberation is considered to be a turning point.

Mandela was elected as the nation's first black president in 1994, which was made possible by the ensuing talks and the breakdown of apartheid, which prepared the path for democratic elections. Resilience of the human spirit in the face of structural injustice is demonstrated by the anti-apartheid struggle, which stands as a tribute to this resilience.

The Vietnam War and the Influence of Ho Chi Minh:

The battle that became known as the Vietnam War was a complicated and drawn-out conflict that sprang with Vietnam's fight for independence from French colonial control. When the Viet Minh were engaged in combat with French soldiers, Ho Chi Minh, a pivotal figure in the anti-colonial movement, was the organization's leader. The battle eventually turned into the Vietnam War, and the United States of America became involved in the conflict in an effort to stop the propagation of communism from spreading.

A great deal of human misery and geopolitical repercussions were brought about as a result of the war, which lasted from 1955 until 1975. Both North and South Vietnam were eventually brought back together in 1976 as a result of the tenacity of the Vietnamese people and their dedication to achieving independence. It is the legacy of Ho Chi Minh that continues to live on as a symbol of Vietnam's fight for self-determination.

Cultural Identities and Nationalism
Regarding the Revival of Language and Culture:

It is not uncommon for the fight for independence to coincide with efforts to resurrect and maintain cultural identities that have been repressed or suppressed as a result of colonial rule. Due to the fact that it functions as a medium of expression, identity, and resistance, language in particular becomes a focal point for the revitalization of cultural traditions.

As a method of claiming separate identities, nationalist organizations frequently place a high priority on the revitalization of indigenous languages, literary works, and cultural activities. This revitalization of language and culture helps to cultivate a sense of belonging and solidarity among communities, which in turn contributes to the larger story of national identity through its contributions.

The Role of Art and Literature in Counterrevolution:

As vehicles for dissent, criticism, and the articulation of national ambitions, artistic expression and literature play a crucial part in the struggle for independence. This is because they serve as vehicles for freedom of expression. Writers, poets, and painters frequently take on the role of torchbearers for the intellectual and artistic aspects of the independence movement.

For instance, the Harlem Renaissance in the United States was not only a cultural movement but also a statement of black identity and resistance against racial injustice. This was something that occurred during the time period. In a similar manner, literary figures such as Rabindranath Tagore and Subhas Chandra Bose utilized their works to motivate and activate the people during India's fight for independence.

Symbolism and National Icons:

Nationalist groups frequently create and embrace symbols and icons that exemplify the spirit of struggle and the pursuit of independence within their respective communities. A sense of togetherness and purpose can be evoked by the use of powerful symbols such as flags, national anthems, and national emblems. In many cases, leaders who emerge victorious from the fight go on to become enduring symbols, recognized for the role they played in determining the destiny of the nation.

A few examples of symbols that are representative of the hardships and aspirations of their respective nations include the Irish tricolor, the Indian tricolor, and the South African flag. Icons such as Che Guevara, who is considered to be a symbol of revolutionary fervor in Latin America, are also examples of people who exemplify the spirit of struggle against oppression.

Obstacles Facing the Nation After Independence
The formation of identities and the building of nations:

At the moment of achieving independence, nations are confronted with the obstacles of state-building and the formation of a national identity. This new chapter marks the beginning of a new chapter. A varied people is brought together into a unified political entity through the process of nation-building, which involves developing the values, institutions, and narratives that bind the population together.

As the nation-building endeavor progresses, questions pertaining to language, ethnicity, religion, and historical narratives become increasingly important. As a result of the negotiation of these components, the contours of national identity are shaped, and citizens' perceptions of themselves and their place within the nation are influenced.

Ethnic and Regional Identities, to Begin with:

Post-independence nations frequently have the challenge of navigating the complexity of ethnic and regional identities that trace back to the time of colonial rule.

Fostering a sense of national unity while also acknowledging and embracing a wide variety of ethnic and regional identities is a difficulty that must be overcome. It is possible that internal conflicts and challenges to the legitimacy of the state could arise if these complications are not successfully addressed.

In post-colonial India, for instance, the existence of a wide variety of languages, faiths, and cultures presented a difficulty to the process of developing a unified national identity. There are still problems with regionalism and identity, despite the fact that the federal structure of the Indian state and the recognition of linguistic diversity through the rearrangement of states have helped to address some of these obstacles.

Economic autonomy

In the post-colonial era, the struggle for economic independence frequently continues, despite the fact that obtaining political independence is a significant milestone. Dependence on previous colonial powers, unequal distribution of resources, and the legacy of exploitative economic systems are all potential economic issues that may be faced by countries that were formerly colonized.

Efforts to attain economic independence include the development of economies that are capable of supporting themselves, the reduction of dependence on foreign aid, and the resolution of concerns pertaining to differences in wealth. When it comes to ensuring long-term sovereignty, the ability to control and manage economic resources eventually becomes an essential component.

An intricate and multi-faceted journey that encompasses historical, political, cultural, and social elements, the fight for independence and identity is a journey that is both complicated and multifaceted. Beginning with the struggle against colonial control and continuing through the difficulties of nation-building and post-colonial governance, this conflict is responsible for shaping the fates of both communities and nations.

When leaders and movements are inspired with the spirit of resistance, they become agents of change and symbolize the aspirations of those who are seeking autonomy. It is through the struggle for independence that cultural identities, which were frequently repressed under colonial authority, are able to find expression and resurgence, contributing to the rich tapestry of global diversity.

It is necessary for nations to traverse the complexity of identity, governance, and economic viability in order to survive the post-independence era, which brings its own set of obstacles. The continual search of justice, equality, and self-determination continues to be an essential component of the developing narratives of independence and identity in the modern world.

As the international community contemplates the historical wars for independence, it is of the utmost importance to acknowledge the ongoing significance of these tales in defining the present and determining the trajectories of nations and the people who live inside them. It is a monument to the human spirit's potential for resilience, endurance, and the desire of a more just and equitable world that the struggle for independence and identity stands as a testament to these qualities.

6.1 Overview of the nationalist movement and its impact on the naming discourse

A phenomena that gathered speed in the latter half of the 19th century and the early 20th century, the nationalist movement is a powerful and transformational force that plays a significant role in molding the destinies of nations because of its influence. Nationalist movements originated as a reaction to colonial control, imperial dominance, and harsh governance. These movements were founded on the aspiration for self-determination, cultural autonomy, and political independence. The purpose of this investigation is to present an overview of the nationalist movement and its enormous impact on the discourse around naming. This impact includes the renaming of places, the revival of indigenous languages, and the assertion of cultural identities.

The Beginnings of Nationalism

The Colonial Context:

The origins of nationalist movements may be traced back to the colonial era, which was characterized by the establishment of imperial dominance over enormous regions by European powers. The colonial experience was defined by the imposition of foreign languages and administrative institutions, as well as the subordination of cultural traditions and the cultivation of exploitation. During the time that indigenous peoples were subjected to the effects of colonial control, feelings of dissatisfaction, resistance, and a desire for independence began to emerge.

The Foundations of Intellectualism:

Thinkers, scholars, and leaders who defined the ideals of self-determination and national identity created the intellectual groundwork for nationalism. These individuals laid the foundations at the intellectual level. A number of intellectual movements, including the European Enlightenment, were instrumental in the development of concepts such as democracy, individual rights, and the idea of a nation-state.

The discourse on nationalism was influenced by the writings of authors such as Jean-Jacques Rousseau, Giuseppe Mazzini, and Johann Gottfried Herder, and these texts helped to create a shared consciousness across many communities.

Increasing Numbers of Political Movements:

During the latter half of the 19th century and the early part of the 20th century, some political movements emerged with the objective of transforming nationalist sentiments into tangible deeds. When it was established in 1885, the Indian National Congress became a focal point for the nationalist movement in India that was fighting against the control of the British colonial government. The same thing happened in different parts of Africa, Asia, and the Middle East: movements for independence and self-determination began about the same time.

There were many different tactics that were utilized by nationalist movements. These tactics included political activism, civil disobedience, armed resistance, and cultural rebirth. The assertion of the right to select one's own political destiny, free from the influence of other forces, was the common objective of all of these movements.

Changing the Names of Locations

Retention of Symbolic Meaning:

The renaming of locations became a real and symbolic manifestation of the ambitions of nationalists toward their homeland. This resulted in the erasure of indigenous toponyms and cultural references. Colonial rulers frequently imposed names that represented their cultural and imperial tastes onto their subjects. Therefore, the process of renaming represented a reclaiming of cultural identity, a rejection of colonial impositions, and an assertion of sovereignty within the community.

During the nationalist movement in India, for example, the renaming of towns, streets, and landmarks became an important component of the campaign. The cities of Bombay, Madras, and Calcutta were renamed as Mumbai, Chennai, and Kolkata, respectively. In order to break away from the legacy of colonialism, these alterations were made with the intention of restoring indigenous names, which frequently reflect historical or cultural value.

Cultural Significance:

The process of renaming locations was not only an exercise in language or administration; rather, it was extremely significant from a cultural and historical perspective. Native American names frequently carried with them stories, legends, and customs that were associated with the area.

Nationalist organizations tried to reestablish these names in order to reestablish a connection with their cultural roots, cultivate a sense of pride and ownership, and combat the cultural erasure that was imposed by colonial powers.

For instance, the renaming of African towns after independence, such as the transformation of Rhodesia to Zimbabwe, signified a deliberate effort to shed colonial legacies and adopt names that reflected the indigenous heritage and efforts for liberation. This was done in order to honor the people who had fought for their freedom.

Declarations of Political Opinion:

The renaming of locations served not only as historical markers but also as political declarations, indicating a departure from the past and the development of new political orders. It asserted the right of nations to construct their own identities and determine the narratives that are linked with their geographical areas, thus conveying a sense of agency and autonomy to the people.

The process of renaming locations frequently occurred concurrently with the larger endeavor of nation-building, which played a role in the formation of a collective sense of national identity. Renaming became a powerful instrument for creating the communal memory and forging a sense of oneness among many populations. This was accomplished through the change of names.

The revival of indigenous languages

Language as a Means of Manifesting One's Identity:

Movements that were nationalist acknowledged the significance of language as a medium through which identity, communication, and cultural expression might be expressed. Indigenous languages were frequently pushed to the background as a result of colonial powers' efforts to impose their own languages, which contributed to the loss of linguistic variety. As a means of recovering cultural autonomy and affirming separate identities, the nationalist response included a rebirth of indigenous languages as a medium of communication.

The Gaelic Revival was an ongoing movement in Ireland that aimed to revitalize the Irish language as an essential component of Irish national identity. A revitalized appreciation for the linguistic legacy was fostered through the promotion of the use of Irish in education, literature, and public discourse. This was done in an effort to challenge the dominance of English in these areas.

Reforms to the Language:

Language reforms were commonly advocated for by nationalist organizations, with the goal of establishing indigenous languages as official languages and mediums of teaching. The overarching objective of decolonization was to challenge the language hierarchy that was imposed by colonial rulers and to restore linguistic equality. Language reforms were an essential component of this overarching goal.

Language policies in post-colonial India were designed to acknowledge and encourage the country's diverse linguistic landscape. Additionally, the recognition of regional languages, in addition to the acceptance of Hindi and English as official languages, demonstrated a commitment to linguistic plurality and the accommodation of a variety of linguistic identities.

Preserving the Cultural Heritage of the Community:

There was a strong connection between the preservation of cultural assets and the revival of indigenous languages. The collective knowledge, folklore, and cultural subtleties of a group are included in the language that is spoken within that community.

The revitalization of indigenous languages functioned as a means of maintaining cultural information and passing it along from one generation to the next.

In the context of greater cultural revival movements, efforts were made to document, standardize, and promote indigenous languages. Language academies, literary organizations, and educational programs that are centered on language were some of the initiatives that were undertaken with the intention of ensuring the continuity of cultural traditions that are embedded in linguistic expressions.

The Proclamation of Cultural Identities

Movements Within the Cultural Revival:

Cultural revival movements, which attempted to recover, commemorate, and renew indigenous cultural practices, were frequently initiated by nationalist movements. Through the use of traditional art forms, music, dance, and rituals, people were able to proclaim their cultural identities and fight against the impacts of colonialism, which were characterized by homogenization.

In Mexico, the time following the revolution was marked by the promotion of indigenous art, particularly through the murals created by Diego Rivera and other artists. As a result of these paintings, indigenous history, culture, and struggle were recognized, which contributed to the formation of a distinct Mexican identity that included both indigenous and mestizo roots.

Reevaluating the Narratives of the Nation:

Within the context of nationalist movements, the process of redefining national narratives went hand in hand with the assertion of cultural identities. The stories, myths, and symbols that had a significant impact on the collective imagination were reinterpreted, with a particular emphasis placed on narratives that highlighted the achievements of indigenous people, the struggles for independence, and the resiliency of local cultures.

An example of this would be the Maori Renaissance in New Zealand, which entailed the reclaiming of Maori identity, language, and traditional practices. There was a renaissance of traditional waka (canoe) building, the haka, and traditional tattooing (ta moko), all of which became significant symbols of Maori cultural pride.

Confronting the Obstacles of Inclusivity:

In spite of the fact that nationalist groups sought to assert cultural identities, they also had difficulties in ensuring that they were inclusive. There are many countries that are distinguished by the presence of a wide variety of cultural, linguistic, and ethnic groups. The process of developing a national identity requires successfully navigating the challenges of diversity.

Careful discussion was required in order to achieve a balance between the development of a national identity and the recognition of regional and ethnic diversity in countries such as India and Nigeria. A sense of national unity must be fostered without eliminating or marginalizing the cultural differences that exist among the various populations. This is the problem that must be overcome.

The nationalist movement, which places a strong focus on self-determination, cultural autonomy, and political independence, has left an indelible effect on the debate surrounding the naming of nations. Some of the concrete manifestations of the larger struggle for independence include the renaming of places, the revival of indigenous languages, and the assertion of cultural identities.

The influence of nationalist movements extends beyond the immediate era following independence, and it continues to have an effect on continuing discussions regarding national identity, language regulations, and the preservation of cultural traditions. The complex and ever-evolving character of the naming debate in the modern world is highlighted by the difficulties that arise when attempting to strike a balance between the statement of a national identity and the promotion of inclusivity.

As nations continue to struggle with issues pertaining to their identities, languages, and cultural heritage, the legacy of the nationalist movement serves as a source of inspiration, a place for reflection, and a forum for ongoing conversation. It is possible to get significant insights into the processes of cultural resilience, identity development, and the ongoing drive for self-determination through the investigation of the impact that nationalist ideology has had on the debate surrounding naming names.

6.2 Discussion on the use of "India" as a symbol of unity during the independence movement

There was a purposeful and strategic choice taken by leaders and activists during the independence movement to adopt the name "India" as a symbol of unification. This choice was made in order to establish a unified national identity in the face of colonial control. As a result of its rich cultural heritage and varied historical context, the phrase evolved into a unifying force that transcended distinctions in language, religion, and geographical location. The intention of this conversation is to investigate the significance of the term "India" as a symbol of unity during the independence movement. More specifically, it will investigate the ways in which it played a role in the mobilization of many populations, the negotiation of identities, and the envisioning of a communal future.

Contextualization of the Past

The Fragmentation of Colonialism:

The Indian subcontinent was characterized by a complex patchwork of princely states, linguistic diversity, and religious pluralism prior to the nationalist movement gaining steam in the late 19th and early 20th centuries. This was the case before the nationalist movement gained traction. The British colonial presence further worsened divisions by utilizing techniques of "divide and rule" in order to keep control over the various populations by dividing them into distinct groups.

During the time that leaders were trying to organize against the common oppressor, it became important that they have a collective identity that is capable of transcending these differentiations. The term "India" was used in a deliberate manner in order to conjure up a common historical and cultural heritage that had the potential to bring together the many communities in their pursuit of independence.

In the beginning, there was a national consciousness

Intellectual movements, socioeconomic shifts, and cultural revitalization all contributed to the development of a nascent national consciousness in the latter half of the 19th century.

The development of a sense of common identity and pride across many communities was significantly aided by the contributions of individuals such as Raja Ram Mohan Roy, Dadabhai Naoroji, and Swami Vivekananda.

After its founding in 1885, the Indian National Congress transformed into a forum for the expression of political demands and the promotion of unity among political leaders hailing from a variety of geographical areas and linguistic backgrounds. Nevertheless, the difficulty remained in locating a symbol that could be used to unite the masses and transcend the myriad of identities that existed at the time.

The Symbolic Importance of the Word "India"
Continuity in Historical and Cultural Backgrounds:

"India" is a phrase that contains significant historical and cultural meanings, since it represents a continuity of culture that precedes the age of colonialism. Using this historical legacy as a means of highlighting the fact that the subcontinent possessed a rich and ancient tradition that predated the period of colonial dominance, nationalist leaders attempted to underline the significance of this heritage.

It was via references to ancient civilizations, such as the Indus Valley Civilization, as well as the contributions of intellectuals such as Aryabhata and Panini, that the concept of a continuous cultural identity that had persisted for millennia was strengthened. Through the use of the word "India" as a symbol, the goal was to establish a connection between the fight for independence and a more comprehensive historical narrative that emphasized resiliency, knowledge, and cultural accomplishments.

Unity of Geography:

Additionally, the word "India" served to emphasize the geographical similarities that exist within the subcontinent. India was conceived of as a single geographical entity with natural boundaries, despite the fact that it possesses a substantial amount of linguistic and cultural variety. This geographic homogeneity served as a rallying point, highlighting the fact that the various villages and areas were all a part of a bigger whole.

A sense of geographic inclusion was fostered by the multitude of landscapes that were there, which ranged from the Himalayas to the Deccan Plateau, from the Gangetic plains to the coastal regions. The name "India" was used to represent a common homeland that included the many ecosystems and terrains, which helped to cultivate a sense of shared destiny among the people who lived there.

The Diversity of Linguistics:

There were a great number of languages and dialects spoken across the various parts of the Indian subcontinent, which contributed to the tremendous linguistic diversity that existed on this continent. In order to use the word "India" as a symbol of unity, it was necessary to resolve the linguistic complications and make certain that the multiplicity of languages did not become a source of division.

During the course of the nationalist debate, influential figures such as Mahatma Gandhi acknowledged the significance of linguistic inclusion. A number of different languages were accommodated within the framework of a unified India through the efforts that were undertaken. In the case of Gandhi, for example, he fought for the recognition of Hindi, Urdu, and other significant languages while simultaneously highlighting the importance of respecting the plurality of languages.

Political Mobilization and Inclusivity

Regarding Political Platforms:

It was during the time of the independence movement that the phrase "India" became an essential component of political platforms and manifestos. The idea of a unified India was a prominent motif that was utilized by the Indian National Congress, which served as a representative body of the nationalist movement. Within the framework of a unified India, the demands for self-governance, constitutional reforms, and an end to colonial exploitation were framed at the same time.

The concept of India was utilized as a rallying cry by political leaders in order to galvanize public support for the fight against colonial authority. Not only did slogans such as "Quit India" resonate as a call for the departure of the British, but they also resonated as a cry for the emancipation of the entire subcontinent.

Communities that are welcoming to all:

The usage of the word "India" as a symbol of unity was an attempt to be inclusive of the various religious, ethnic, and cultural groupings that were found on the subcontinent. It was understood by the leaders that there was a need to build a collective identity that could transcend sectarian ties and to reconcile the religious divides that existed.

The secular element of the Indian identity was highlighted by prominent figures such as Jawaharlal Nehru, who envisioned a society in which individuals of varying religious and cultural origins could coexist peacefully. Within the framework of the nationalist narrative, the concept of India as a nation that is both pluralistic and inclusive emerged as a focal point.

Identities are being negotiated

Within the context of a more comprehensive national identity, the process of utilizing "India" as a symbol of unification required the negotiation of many identities. The leaders actively engaged in conversation and debate in order to successfully negotiate the intricate interaction of linguistic, religious, and regional identities. To create a sense of togetherness without eliminating the rich tapestry of diversity that marked the subcontinent was the problem that needed to be overcome.

The formulation of a constitution, the establishment of a national song, and the adoption of a national flag were all symbolic gestures that were made with the intention of recognizing and incorporating a variety of identities into the overarching concept of India.

Obstacles and Criticisms

The Regional Goals and Objectives:

In spite of the fact that the usage of "India" as a symbol of unity was mostly successful in rousing a collective opposition against colonial control, it was also confronted with obstacles from regional desires. Depending on their linguistic or ethnic identity, certain regions aimed to achieve more autonomy or perhaps become their own independent nation.

The demand for linguistic states in the post-independence era, such as the restructuring of states in India in 1956, reflected the ongoing negotiation between the concept of a united India and the recognition of regional identities. This negotiation includes the recognition of regional identities. The federal structure of the Indian state was designed with the intention of striking a balance between the requirement for a centralized identity and the necessity to accommodate regional differences.

Post-colonial identity

The term "India" continued to be used as a symbol of unity well into the post-colonial era; yet, the difficulties of developing a national identity that is distinct and coherent continued to exist. In the course of ongoing discussions over the nature of Indian identity, the complexity of linguistic, religious, and ethnic variety continued to play a significant role.

Certain tribes and places were excluded or marginalized, according to critics, because the phrase "India" frequently indicated a historical and cultural continuity that excluded or marginalized them. The continual complications of negotiating unity and diversity were brought to light by efforts to assert linguistic, ethnic, or regional identities within the context of the larger Indian identity.

Reflections on the Present Day World
Pluralism Based on Culture:

The concept of "India" as a symbol of togetherness is continuously evolving in modern-day India, with continuing arguments regarding cultural pluralism, variety, and inclusivity serving as the driving forces behind this evolution. The acknowledgment of regional cuisines, the celebration of a variety of festivals, and the recognition of multiple languages all contribute to a more comprehensive sense of Indian identity that celebrates the country's diversity.

It is widely acknowledged that the wider narrative of a unified India is inextricably linked to the preservation and promotion of indigenous languages, the protection of cultural heritage, and the celebration of regional identities. The commitment to a democratic, secular, and inclusive nation is reflected in the Constitution of India, which was enacted in the year 1950.

The Obstacles Facing Unity in the Face of Diversity:

When attempting to capture the essence of India's identity, the phrase "Unity in Diversity" is frequently utilized. On the other hand, maintaining a harmonious balance between unity and variety continues to be a difficulty that must be overcome. Language, religion, caste, and regional disparities continue to be issues of contention and controversy. Other sources of friction include regional differences.

The modern debate on Indian identity must include key components such as efforts to resolve historical injustices, create social equity, and strengthen populations that have been disenfranchised. The problem is in bringing together the varied goals of more than a billion people in India within the context of a common vision for the country.

A strategic and pragmatic choice that intended to unify a varied subcontinent against colonial rule, the adoption of "India" as a symbol of unity during the independence movement was a choice that was made in order to achieve this specific goal. The word served as a rallying point, conjuring historical continuity, geographic homogeneity, and a cultural history that was shared by all.

Despite the fact that it was successful in rallying a collective opposition, the difficulties of negotiating identities, accommodating diversity, and encouraging tolerance continue to exist in the modern period.

The road that India took from being a colonial oppression to becoming an independent nation was filled with the challenges of both unity and diversity. The dynamic nature of a nation that is still working through the complexity of its history, culture, and society is reflected in the continuous conversation over Indian identity. As India struggles to come to terms with the challenges of the 21st century, the symbolism of "India" as a force that brings people together continues to be an essential component of the nation's self-perception and its position on the international scene.

6.3 Examination of debates surrounding the choice of a national identity

It is a complicated and multi-faceted process that requires the negotiation of historical, cultural, linguistic, and socio-political aspects in order to arrive at a decision regarding a national identity. Nations struggle with the dilemma of how to define themselves, debating whether or not to place an emphasis on a shared past, a similar culture, linguistic relations, or a political ideology. The purpose of this investigation is to investigate the discussions that surround the selection of a national identity. It investigates the difficulties, conflicts, and ramifications of the decisions that shape the collective sense of self that exists inside a nation.

Contextualization of the Past

The development of contemporary nations:

The development of modern nations frequently entails a process of identity construction that is both planned and, at times, contentious at the same time. When nations are forced to define their identities as separate political entities as a result of historical events such as wars, revolutions, or the fall of empires, they are forced to do so. During this process, decisions must be made regarding the inclusion or exclusion of particular groups, the choosing of symbols and narratives, and the establishment of cultural and language standards.

The aftermath of World War I and the fall of empires such as the Ottoman Empire and the Austro-Hungarian Empire led to the formation of new nation-states in Europe. These new nation-states were each faced with the issue of developing a national identity that reflected the ambitions and histories of their respective populations. As states emerged from colonial domination, nations in Asia, Africa, and the Americas went through procedures that were almost identical.

Post-colonial identity

When it comes to post-colonial situations, the selection of a national identity is frequently closely connected to the fight for independence and the aspiration to express cultural sovereignty. The legacies of forced identities, linguistic impositions, and the erasure of indigenous cultures leave colonized nations unable to cope with the aftermath of colonization. The post-colonial period is a crucial crossroads for nations to reinvent themselves. During this time, nations frequently engage in disputes regarding whether components of their pre-colonial legacy should be emphasized and how to handle the complexities of cultural variety.

In India, for example, the time following the country's independence was marked by the negotiation of linguistic diversity, regional identities, and the task of building a united national identity. The continuous discussions concerning post-colonial identity creation are reflected in the efforts that are being made to accommodate linguistic and regional diversity while still preserving a feeling of national unity.

Considerations Regarding the Cultural, Linguistic, and Religious Aspects Identities of the Culture:

In the process of selecting cultural aspects to serve as markers of national identity, it is common practice to select symbols, customs, and historical narratives that are meaningful to a large cross-section of the community. It is possible for nations to choose to place an emphasis on particular cultural practices, artistic expressions, or historical events that are regarded as being representative of the distinctive personality of the nation.

As an illustration, the cultural identity of Japan is frequently linked to customs and practices such as tea ceremonies, cherry blossom festivals, and ancient handicrafts such as ikebana and calligraphy. The Japanese national identity is characterized by a sense of continuity and distinctiveness, both of which are contributed to by these cultural components.

Identity in Linguistics:

Language makes a significant contribution to the formation of national identity. The selection of an official language or languages, the establishment of linguistic policy, and the use of symbols related to language can have significant repercussions for the principles of inclusion and representation within a nation. Due to the fact that languages carry within them the histories, values, and expressions of a people, discussions about language frequently overlap with a variety of concerns concerning cultural identity.

In nations such as Canada, where both English and French are recognized as official languages, the existence of linguistic duality is a manifestation of the efforts made to accommodate the many different languages spoken by the population. However, linguistic choices can also be causes of tension, particularly in multilingual cultures where distinct language communities want acknowledgment and representation. This particularly occurs in civilizations where there are multiple languages.

Identifying with a Religious Group:

Religion is a significant factor in determining the identity of many nations, and it frequently has an impact on the cultural traditions, ethical standards, and social structures of those nations. A nation's character can be shaped by the selection of a dominant religion or by the acknowledgment of several religions as part of the national identity. This can also have an effect on the rights and freedoms of religious communities.

One of the most important aspects of national identity in nations such as Saudi Arabia and Iran is Islam, which has a significant impact on the legal systems, social standards, and cultural expressions of such countries. In contrast, countries such as India, which have a rich tapestry of religious variety, face the issue of tolerating multiple religious identities within a framework that prioritizes secularism.

The Political and Ideological Aspects of the Situation

Political Identities:

The fundamental concepts, values, and administrative institutions that characterize a nation are the foundation upon which political identity is built. One of the most important factors that contributes to the formation of a nation's identity is the political system that is chosen, whether it be democratic, authoritarian, socialist, or another. In the process of political identity development, political symbols, institutions, and historical narratives that are associated with the fight for independence or political transition become essential components.

For instance, the United States of America places a strong emphasis on democratic principles, the Constitution, and the founding fathers as essential components of its own political identity. The concept of a government that is "of the people, by the people, and for the people" has emerged as a fundamental principle of the political identity of the United States of America.

Ideological Identity:

A nation's worldview is shaped by its ideological identity, which is composed of the guiding ideas and beliefs that define that worldview.

There are many instances in which nations define particular ideas that serve as the basis for legislation, diplomatic relations, and societal ideals. Whatever ideology a nation chooses to adhere to—whether it be nationalism, socialism, liberalism, or another ideology—it has the potential to influence both its internal and international direction.

China's acceptance of socialism with Chinese features under the leadership of the Communist Party represents an ideological decision that unites socialist ideals with a commitment to economic reforms and modernization. This choice was made by China. The formation of national narratives and the ascertainment of a nation's place in the global community are both influenced by the ideological choices that are made.

Obstacles and Debates in the Discussion

The Difference Between Inclusivity and Exclusivity:

Choosing a national identity presents a number of obstacles, one of the most significant of which is finding a middle ground between inclusiveness and exclusivity. In many cases, nations are confronted with the challenge of defining a national identity that acknowledges and celebrates variety while also avoiding the suppression of particular groups. National identities that are inclusive accept and cherish variety, thereby acknowledging the contributions that many communities have made to the distinct personality of the nation over time.

On the other hand, national identities that tend to be exclusive may give priority to particular cultural, linguistic, or religious characteristics, which may result in the marginalization of minority groups. When it comes to maintaining social cohesion and ensuring that varied views are provided with an equal representation inside the nation, striking a balance becomes absolutely essential.

Narratives of Historical Events:

There are many competing historical narratives at the center of discussions regarding the selection of a national identity. It is possible for a nation's collective memory to be shaped by the choosing of particular historical personalities, events, and cultural landmarks. When different groups within a nation have differing interpretations of historical events or when they question the narratives offered by the state, this can give birth to situations that are characterized by controversy.

For instance, disagreements over historical narratives are prevalent in nations that have had a complicated colonial past.

In these nations, different points of view on the fight for independence or the effects of colonial rule can eventually result in national identities that are in contradiction with one another.

Identities of Regional and Ethnic Community:

Those on national identity sometimes cross with those about regional and ethnic identities, particularly in nations that have a varied range of linguistic, cultural, or ethnic minorities. One of the challenges is to develop a sense of national unity while also understanding and respecting the differences that exist between regions. A more inclusive national identity can be achieved by the implementation of policies that either acknowledge the rights of ethnic minorities or allow for the autonomy of regional communities.

The acknowledgment of regional identities, such as Catalonia and the Basque Country, has been a topic of ongoing controversy in Spain, for instance. Catalonia falls under the category of regional identities. In order to strike a balance between regional sovereignty and a more comprehensive Spanish identity, it is necessary to navigate the intricate historical and cultural forces.

Hybrid Identities and the Impact of Globalization
Impacts from Around the World:

In the context of discussions concerning national identity, the period of globalization has brought about the introduction of new dynamics. The merging of global and local impacts has occurred as a result of increased connectedness, migration, and the flow of information. Countries are required to face the problems of preserving their own national identities while also engaging with the cultural, economic, and political developments that are occurring on a global scale.

The proliferation of global media, the existence of the internet, and the movement of cultural ideas across international borders all contribute to the development of hybrid identities that combine aspects of both local and global cultures. The process of selecting a national identity becomes intricately entangled with the challenges of navigating global influences and maintaining cultural authenticity.

Appropriation of Cultural Practices:

Concerns regarding cultural appropriation, which occurs when components of a nation's culture are commodified or exploited by actors from outside the nation due to globalization, have also arisen as a result of globalization. When it comes to maintaining their cultural history and making sure that depictions of their identity in the global arena are accurate and respectful, nations may confront obstacles.

It is possible for tensions and disagreements to arise around the preservation of cultural integrity when global entities inappropriately appropriate indigenous symbols, traditional garb, or religious traditions without having the necessary understanding or context.

The complex and ever-changing nature of identity development within nations is shown by the disputes that surround the selection of a national identity. The narratives that bind different communities together into a sense of common belonging are shaped by the decisions that are made about the cultural, linguistic, religious, political, and ideological components.

Despite the fact that nations are currently navigating the issues of inclusivity, historical interpretations, regional diversity, and global influences, the ongoing conversation concerning national identity continues to be a crucial and dynamic component of contemporary discourse. Throughout the years to come, the decisions that nations make in defining and redefining their identities will continue to be influenced by their capacity to strike a balance between unity and diversity, to accept the complexities of history, and to engage with the realities of the global community.

Chapter 7

Post-Independence: India on the Global Stage

An important turning point in the history of India occurred in the years immediately after the country's attainment of independence in 1947. India proceeded on a journey of nation-building, economic development, and global involvement at the same time that the world witnessed the formation of a new sovereign state. Indian foreign policy, economic issues, diplomatic contacts, and evolving involvement in international events are all topics that are investigated in this investigation, which digs into India's post-independence trajectory on the world arena.

The Foundational Principles of International Relations

Non-Alignment:

The ideas of non-alignment, which were defined by Jawaharlal Nehru, India's first Prime Minister, were the most influential in shaping India's foreign policy after the country gained its independence. The objective of non-alignment was to preserve independence from the blocs that existed during the Cold War, to encourage strategic autonomy, and to promote peaceful cohabitation. In order to successfully navigate the global power dynamics, India strived to avoid associating itself with either the Western or Eastern blocs, which were respectively led by the United States of America and the Soviet Union.

India was able to pursue an autonomous foreign policy agenda, with an emphasis on diplomacy, disarmament, and economic development, thanks to its relationship with non-aligned nations. It was during the Bandung Conference in 1955 that India expressed this position, which was later codified in the Non-Aligned Movement (NAM). This position placed India as a significant actor in the worldwide pursuit of peace and development throughout the world.

Principles of the Panchsheel Order:

Additionally, India advocated for the Panchsheel principles, which are a set of guiding principles for international relations that are based on mutual respect, non-interference, and peaceful coexistence. Non-alignment was another value that India supported. The Panchsheel agreement, which was signed between India and China in 1954, was intended to manage ties between the two Asian nations and placed an emphasis on the need of settling problems through peaceful methods.

In spite of the fact that the Panchsheel principles emphasized India's dedication to discussion and diplomacy, the efficiency of these principles will be put to the test in the years to come by geopolitical changes, notably along the border between India and China.

Challenges Facing the Economy and Opportunities for Development
The Post-Independence Economic Landscape The following:

At the time of its independence, India was confronted with a number of serious economic issues, such as poverty, underdevelopment, and a legacy of colonialism that had left the country economically dependent. The leaders of India, which had recently gained its independence, understood the importance of achieving economic self-sufficiency and hence proceeded on a course of planned economic development.

Since its inception in 1950, the Planning Commission has been responsible for developing a series of Five-Year Plans with the objectives of attaining economic growth, decreasing poverty, and promoting social justice. These programs gave priority to important areas such as agriculture, manufacturing, and infrastructure, thereby laying the framework for the restructuring of India's economy.

In the context of industrialization and mixed economies:

India has embraced a style of economy known as a mixed economy, which has aspects of both socialism and capitalism. The private sector was encouraged to contribute to economic growth, while the public sector played a key role in strategic industries including the military and the aerospace industry. As part of the endeavor to redress historical imbalances and to promote economic inclusion, land reforms and the establishment of large-scale public sector businesses were both implemented.

The process of industrialization gained momentum, with a key emphasis placed on import substitution as a means of reducing reliance on goods imported from other countries. The commitment of the state to promoting the expansion of the industrial sector was demonstrated by the founding of institutions such as the Industrial Development Bank of India (IDBI) and the Steel Authority of India Limited (SAIL).

Amendments to the Agricultural System and the Green Revolution:

The Green Revolution was a movement that began in the 1960s with the intention of boosting agricultural production by introducing high-yielding crop varieties, enhancing irrigation systems, and implementing contemporary farming techniques.

Famines were a problem that needed to be addressed, and the success of the Green Revolution led to a rise in food production, which contributed to food security and helped the situation.

A number of agricultural reforms were implemented in later years with the goals of enhancing rural livelihoods, improving land distribution, and modernizing farming practices. Nevertheless, the challenges that are associated with the fragmentation of land, unequal access to resources, and the sustainability of agricultural techniques continue to be significant topics of concern.

Diplomatic Engagements and the Dynamics of the Region
Battles fought with Pakistan:
The post-independence history of India has been marked by a succession of confrontations with Pakistan over territorial issues, particularly in the territories of Jammu and Kashmir. These conflicts have been extremely contentious. Following the initial Indo-Pakistani war that took place in 1947–1948, additional battles took place in 1965 and 1971. Within the context of India's diplomatic and military history, the war that took place in 1971 and resulted in the formation of Bangladesh continues to be a key milestone.

Normalization of relations between India and Pakistan was the goal of the Shimla Agreement of 1972, which was signed after the war that took place in 1971. In addition to reiterating the importance of maintaining the sanctity of the Line of Control in Kashmir, it provided a framework for the resolution of problems through bilateral negotiations.

Relations between China and India:
Over the course of their relationship, India and China have had moments of cooperation, periods of competition, and periods of hostility. During the Sino-Indian War of 1962, territorial conflicts along the Himalayan border were brought to light, which in turn worsened relations between the two nations that dominate Asia. Sino-Indian ties have continued to be shaped by the unsolved border problem as well as the geopolitical competition between the two countries.

The efforts that are being taken to strengthen relations include those that are aimed at fostering confidence, economic collaboration, and diplomatic engagement. Despite this, difficulties continue to exist, and the border dispute continues to be a source of stress, which in turn influences the dynamics of the South Asian region.

The War for the Liberation of Bangladesh:
During the Bangladesh Liberation War in 1971, a significant turning point occurred in the geopolitical landscape of South Asia. Bangladesh was established as a result of India's significant contribution to the independence movement in East Pakistan, which ultimately led to the formation of Bangladesh. In addition, the battle led to conflicts between India and Pakistan as well as the intervention of many international powers.

Both the signing of the Simla Agreement and the return of prisoners of war occurred during the post-war period. These events contributed to the normalization of relations between India and Pakistan, despite the fact that some difficulties continued to exist.

Diplomacy and the Nuclear Program
Nuclear Examinations:
The nuclear program of India and the Pokhran tests that took place in 1974 placed India's nuclear capabilities to the forefront of its international interactions. The tests were carried out as a reaction to the perceived risks to security as well as the shifting

security landscape on a multinational scale. The drive to create nuclear capability was met with scrutiny and condemnation, particularly from the international community.

With a series of nuclear tests conducted at Pokhran in 1998, India's nuclear status was firmly established, notwithstanding the concerns that were raised. At that moment, India's nuclear policy and its approach to global non-proliferation regimes underwent a significant transformation as a result of the tests. Despite the fact that economic penalties were a part of the diplomatic fallout, India made efforts to engage with the international community in order to address concerns and promote nuclear stability over the course of time.

Nuclear Agreement Between India and the United States:

When the United States and India signed the Indo-American Civil Nuclear Agreement in 2008, it marked a key turning point in the relationship between the two countries in the 21st century. The agreement marked a break from India's past nuclear isolation and made it possible for people to work together on nuclear energy projects for civil purposes. The event served as a signal of the developing strategic convergence between the two countries, as well as the acceptance of India as a responsible nuclear state and institution.

India's shifting diplomatic position and its aspirations to build connections with key world powers were reflected in the nuclear accord that was reached between India and the United States.

Liberalization of the Economy and Globalization of the Economy
The Reform of the Economy:

With the implementation of economic liberalization and globalization policies in the early 1990s, India's economic policies underwent a paradigm change that occurred throughout this time period. India, which was experiencing a crisis in its balance of payments, decided to implement market-oriented reforms with the objectives of liberalizing trade, attracting foreign investment, and fostering economic growth.

A significant number of the prior rules that had characterized India's socialist economic model were abolished as a result of the liberalization efforts, which were spearheaded by Manmohan Singh, who was serving as Finance Minister at the time. Through the process of opening up the economy, India was able to become more integrated into the global economy, as well as increase the amount of foreign direct investment and technical breakthroughs.

The explosion of information technology:

The explosion of the information technology (IT) industry was one of the most noteworthy results of the liberalization of international trade. With cities such as Bangalore and Hyderabad becoming important centers for information technology, India has emerged as a global hub for information technology and software services. The outsourcing of software development, business process outsourcing, and information technology services made a substantial contribution to the expansion of India's economy and established the nation as a significant participant in the knowledge economy.

The accomplishments of India's information technology sector demonstrated the country's capacity to compete on a global scale and to make use of its human capital for technological innovation.

Leadership on a Global Scale and Other Multilateral Engagements
Organizations with International Status and the United Nations:

The Indian government has been quite active in participating in international organizations and multilateral forums. Since it was one of the founding members of the United Nations, India has been a staunch supporter of global initiatives that promote fairness, development, and peace. Additionally, the nation has made contributions to United Nations peacekeeping missions, taken part in debates regarding climate change, and actively sought reforms in international institutions in order to better reflect the geopolitical realities of the present century.

A clear indication of India's dedication to influencing the global economic order is the country's leading position in international institutions such as the World Bank, the International Monetary Fund (IMF), and the World Trade Organization (WTO).

Climate Change and the Development of Sustainable Practices:

Through its participation in global efforts to combat climate change and advance sustainable development, India has been a significant contributor. The country's enormous population and rapid economic growth provide issues in terms of the amount of energy that is consumed and the influence that it has on the environment. On the other hand, India has pledged to participate in international partnerships, afforestation programs, and initiatives including renewable energy in order to reduce the effects of climate change.

India has made considerable promises to decrease carbon emissions and transition to a more sustainable and green economy as a result of the Paris Agreement, which was ratified in 2015.

It is a pandemic of COVID-19

The pandemic caused by COVID-19 brought to light the significance of international cooperation in the process of solving common concerns. The provision of drugs, medical supplies, and vaccinations to countries all over the world was a significant contribution made by India as part of the global response. The pandemic brought to light India's dedication to the improvement of public health around the world as well as the importance of international cooperation during times of crisis.

Obstacles and Potential Opportunities
Persistent Security Obstacles:

Terrorism that crossed international borders, insurgencies, and regional conflicts are some of the current security concerns that India must contend with. The danger of terrorist attacks coming from the region has repercussions for India's internal security as well as its relations with the countries that are located in its immediate vicinity.

Maritime problems are also a part of the security landscape, notably in the region surrounding the Indian Ocean, where India is working to preserve its strategic interests and maintain stability.

Geostrategic Dynamics:

The geostrategic location that India has in South Asia and the region surrounding the Indian Ocean places it at the crossroads of the interests of major national powers across the world. India's foreign policy considerations are shaped by the growing dynamics between China and the United States, as well as the dynamics of the region with countries such as Pakistan and Afghanistan.

India is faced with a number of problems and opportunities as it strives to preserve its national interests while simultaneously maintaining a balance between its regional and global activities simultaneously.

Economic Inequalities:

India continues to struggle with persistent economic gaps, social inequality, and poverty, despite the substantial economic progress that has been made. There are still significant problems for the nation to overcome, including bridging the gap between urban and rural areas, resolving income disparity, and guaranteeing equitable growth.

It is also possible for India's economic resilience and growth trajectory to be hindered by global economic concerns, such as the impact of the COVID-19 pandemic.

Following the country's attainment of independence, India's subsequent voyage on the international stage has been characterized by a dynamic interplay of diplomatic engagements, economic reforms, and developing geopolitical realities. India has successfully navigated a complicated global terrain while also establishing its identity as a sovereign nation. This has been accomplished by embracing economic liberalization and adhering to the foundational ideals of non-alignment.

As India continues to establish itself as a key player on the global stage, it is confronted with a wide variety of opportunities and problems. Because of the nation's dedication to multilateralism, sustainable development, and global cooperation, it is in a position to play a significant role in determining the prospects of the international community in the future. The growing position that India plays in the global order of the 21st century is reflected in the country's continued pursuit of national goals while simultaneously cultivating international partnership.

7.1 Exploration of post-independence decisions regarding the country's name

The investigation of judgments made after the country gained its independence about the name of the nation is a fascinating journey through the intricate process of identity creation and the construction of a nation by its citizens. In the case of India, the selection of a name for the newly independent nation was a decision that was both symbolic and momentous, and it brought with it certain connotations that were political, cultural, and historical in nature. In this discussion, we will look into the various causes that played a role in the choice to keep the name "India," as well as the arguments that surrounded alternate names and the larger context of identity in the era after independence.

Some historical context:

At the time of the Indian subcontinent's independence from British colonial authority in 1947, the leaders of the newly formed nation were faced with the tremendous challenge of defining the identity of the nation that had just been formed. The area had a long and illustrious past that included a wide variety of distinct cultures, languages, and religious practices. The selection of a name for the nation was deeply entrenched in the historical consciousness of the people as well as their hopes for a future that is both autonomous and cohesive.

It is believed that the name "India" originates from the River Indus and the civilizations that flourished along its banks. These origins date back to extremely ancient times. Over the course of history, the phrase has been utilized to refer to the entirety of the Indian subcontinent. It was a statement of continuity with the historical tradition of the region that the decision was made to keep the name "India" when the independent nation gained its freedom.

Maintaining a Comprehensible Historical Identity:

The choice to keep the name "India" reflected a deliberate effort to highlight continuity with the historical identity of the subcontinent, which was the motivation behind the decision. The founders of the newly independent nation were aware of the fact that the name "India" had been used for centuries to refer to the geographical and cultural entity that comprised a large and varied territory encompassing a variety of different regions.

By continuing to use the name "India," the leaders of the country wanted to express a sense of historical continuity and resilience in the midst of disruptions caused by colonial rule. The decision was meant to be symbolic of the nation's extensive cultural legacy, ancient civilizations, and the continuing spirit of the people who had inhabited the subcontinent for millennia.

The Diversity of Linguistic and Cultural Expressions:

One of the difficulties that arose during the process of selecting a name for the nation was the need to take into account the linguistic and cultural variety that exists on the Indian subcontinent. The region was home to a great number of languages, each of which had its own script and cultural characteristics. It was possible to achieve inclusion and transcend linguistic divides through the utilization of a phrase such as "India," which was not affiliated with any particular linguistic group and had historical significance.

Alternative suggestions that recommended names based on particular linguistic or regional affiliations were frequently met with opposition despite their potential benefits. In the process of nation-building, the focus placed on a pan-Indian identity, which was reflected in the selection of the name "India," contributed to the narrative that tried to bring together many communities under a common tent.

Nationalist Ideals and the Unity of the Nation:

An ideal of unity in variety was a defining characteristic of the nationalist movement that ultimately resulted in India's attainment of independence. Leaders such as Mahatma Gandhi, Jawaharlal Nehru, and Sardar Patel had the vision of a nation in which individuals of varying religious beliefs, linguistic backgrounds, and cultural traditions could coexist peacefully. The selection of the name "India" as the name for the nation exemplified these same principles of togetherness and harmony.

The necessity for a unified identity became even more apparent in the aftermath of the partition that took place in 1947, which resulted in the Indian subcontinent being split into two independent nations: India and Pakistan. The decision to keep the name "India" emphasized the commitment to a nationhood that is secular and inclusive, and that is capable of transcending religious and regional attachments.

Disputes and Alternative Proposals:

During the formative years of the nation, there were disputes and alternative ideas that appeared, despite the fact that the decision to keep the name "India" was widely accepted by the majority of people. It was a reflection of the many different identities that exist within the subcontinent that some of the alternate names that were suggested had their origins in linguistic or cultural particular aspects.

The notion that the name "Bharat" should be officially adopted as the primary designation for the nation was one example of such a proposal.

With its association with ancient texts and the legendary ruler Bharata, the word "Bharat" has deep origins in the mythology and customs of India. A more indigenous and culturally resonant identity would be reflected, according to those who advocated for this proposition, according to their argument.

The suggestion to use the name "Bharat" as the official name, on the other hand, did not receive much support from that direction. It was decided that the historical continuity linked with the term "India" and the aim to highlight unity were more important than options that would have leaned toward specific language or cultural affiliations.

Position Regarding the Constitution:

Constitutional statement of the decision of the country's name may be found in the Constitution of India, which was initially approved in the year 1950. In the first article of the Constitution, it is stated that "India, which is also known as Bharat, shall be a Union of States." This constitutional provision acknowledges the historical and cultural significance of both titles, which is reflected in the dual nomenclature for the nation, which is "India" and "Bharat."

The inclusion of both names in the Constitution was a pragmatic compromise that acknowledged the variety of linguistic and cultural landscapes that exist inside the nation. "Bharat" found its position in the constitutional discourse, offering a symbolic link to old customs and cultural legacy. This occurred despite the fact that "India" continued to be the term that was recognized worldwide.

Some Reflections on the Present:

It is a reflection of the continuous conflict between historical continuity and emerging identities that the dual nomenclature of "India" and "Bharat" is used in contemporary times. An official designation for diplomatic, political, and economic connections, the label "India" is firmly established in international discourse. It serves as the official designation for these interactions. On the other hand, the term "Bharat" continues to serve as a cultural and symbolic reference within the scope of the constitution.

Using both names is a reflection of the nuanced attitude to identification that is prevalent in India, a country in which historical legacies coexist with the imperatives of a society that is both dynamic and varied. The constitutional acknowledgment of both names makes it possible to have a multifaceted conception of the identity of the nation, which takes into account the complexity of both linguistic and cultural variety as well as historical diversity.

A multidimensional process that was impacted by historical, cultural, and political concerns is revealed when one investigates the decisions that were made after the country gained its independence about the name of the nation. The decision to keep the name "India" was one that was made on purpose in order to place an emphasis on historical continuity, inclusivity, and the idea of a nation that is both cohesive and varied.

The choice to keep the name "India" demonstrated a dedication to a pan-Indian identity that transcended linguistic and regional ties. This was despite the fact that alternative options were presented. The constitutional recognition of both "India" and "Bharat" makes it possible to have a nuanced understanding of the identity of the nation. This acknowledges the rich tapestry of history and culture that characterizes the Indian subcontinent. India is a nation that is always evolving in the 21st century, and the dual nomenclature serves as a reminder of the ongoing debate between tradition and modernity, unity and diversity, which is what defines the identity of the nation.

7.2 Analysis of how "India" gained international recognition

The story of how "India" came to be recognized on a worldwide scale is a tale that is intricately connected with the nation's fight for independence, diplomatic endeavors, and its position in international affairs. India's efforts to establish itself as a recognized and respected entity on the international stage were marked by diplomatic acumen, principled foreign policy, and a commitment to peaceful coexistence. These efforts began in the early 20th century, when the concept of self-rule gained momentum, and continued through the post-independence period. The purpose of this analysis is to investigate the significant milestones, problems, and methods that have led to India's achievements on the world stage.

Diplomacy Involved Prior to Independence:

Already prior to India's attainment of independence in 1947, the leaders of the Indian nationalist movement were actively involved in diplomatic efforts to obtain support from the world community for their cause. On a variety of international forums, figures such as Mahatma Gandhi and Jawaharlal Nehru, among others, endeavored to convey India's aspirations for self-determination and emancipation from colonial authority.

The Indian National Congress and its leaders played a significant part in the process of creating awareness about the Indian independence movement on a global scale.

This was accomplished by visiting international conferences, connecting with leaders from around the world, and explaining India's position on self-rule. Nehru, who went on to become India's first Prime Minister, was one of the figures who played a significant role in building the basis for India's diplomatic contacts after the country gained its independence.

Diplomacy in the Years Following Independence:
Regarding the membership of the United Nations:

The acquisition of India's membership in the United Nations (UN) was one of the earliest diplomatic achievements for the newly independent nation of India. In spite of the fact that India had not yet achieved its independence, it joined the United Nations on October 30, 1945. When it came to gaining international recognition for the newly constituted nation, the contributions of influential individuals such as Vijaya Lakshmi Pandit, who was India's envoy to the United Nations, were of fundamental importance.

The commencement of India's active involvement in international issues may be traced back to the country's membership in the United Nations. India is now a significant player in the international diplomatic arena as a result of Nehru's focus on values such as non-alignment and his dedication to a just international order. These principles resonated with many nations that had recently gained their independence.

Non-Alignment and Leadership in the Global Community:

The non-alignment foreign strategy that Jawaharlal Nehru advocated for became a distinguishing characteristic of India's position in the international arena. At the Bandung Conference in 1955, the concept of non-alignment was created with the intention of preserving independence from the Cold War blocs, increasing collaboration among developing nations, and supporting disarmament. India became a leader of the non-aligned movement while Nehru was in charge of the country, which helped to strengthen India's status as a significant player in the geopolitical affairs of the world.

Nehru's diplomatic encounters with leaders such as Gamal Abdel Nasser of Egypt, Sukarno of Indonesia, and Josip Broz Tito of Yugoslavia contributed to the formation of coalitions that transcended ideological differences. By adhering to the principle of non-alignment, India was able to maintain the flexibility to engage with nations that spanned the whole political spectrum, which contributed to the country's expanding prominence on the international stage.

The crisis in Suez and the resolution that was reached in the United Nations:

India's diplomatic participation during the Suez Crisis of 1956 proved the country's dedication to the peaceful resolution of international disputes through the use of conflict resolution strategies. Nehru's decision to adopt a stance against military aggression was spurred by the crisis that involved the invasion of the Suez Canal by Israel, the United Kingdom, and France.

The United Nations General Assembly passed a resolution that demanded an immediate ceasefire and the evacuation of foreign forces. India was a significant contributor to the organization's success in gaining support for this resolution. The resolution was successfully passed, which brought to light India's diplomatic capabilities as well as its dedication to maintaining the values of international law and peace.

A recognition of the Republic of India

The recognition of the Republic of India as a sovereign and independent state was an essential step in the process of attaining international recognition. It was necessary to engage in diplomatic activities in order to obtain formal recognition from other countries during the process of transitioning from being a British colony to an independent republic.

When India gained its independence, the United States of America was one of the first countries to acknowledge it. On August 15, 1947, the day that India gained its independence, President Harry S. Truman extended recognition to the country. India's status as a sovereign entity in the world community was established as a result of this diplomatic gesture, which paved the way for India to seek recognition from other nations.

Economic Diplomacy and Partnerships for Development:
Reforms to the Economy and Integration Across the World:

The period following India's independence was marked by the implementation of economic reforms and the country's efforts to integrate itself into the global economy. India's approach to matters pertaining to foreign economic relations underwent a substantial transformation as a result of the economic liberalization policies that were implemented in the early 1990s.

The economic diplomacy of India consisted of a number of important components, including the opening of the economy to foreign investment, the reduction of trade obstacles, and participation in global trade conferences. A significant factor that contributed to India's improved standing on the international scene was the country's incorporation into the existing economic order of the world.

Collaboration between South-South Countries and Partnerships for Development:

Specifically with countries located in the Global South, India actively participated in the formation of development partnerships with other nations. In order to solve shared difficulties and advance sustainable development, the notion of South-South cooperation placed an emphasis on the collaboration that exists between developing nations' efforts.

The contributions that India has made to technical cooperation, capacity-building, and assistance in fields like agriculture and healthcare have helped to create its reputation as a responsible and beneficent operator in the field of international development. A number of initiatives, such as the Indian Technical and Economic Cooperation (ITEC) program and the founding of the Indian Development and Economic Assistance Scheme (IDEAS), contributed to India's increased engagement with national governments from other countries.

Nuclear Diplomacy:
Pokhran Tests and Responses from Around the World:

The international respect that India has received is largely attributable to the nuclear diplomacy that it has engaged in. The nuclear missile tests that were carried out at Pokhran in 1974 were a watershed moment in the history of India's nuclear strategy. Following the tests, a variety of states throughout the world responded in a variety of ways. Some nations voiced their concerns about the proliferation of nuclear weapons, while others acknowledged India's security imperatives.

The Comprehensive Nuclear Test Ban Treaty (CTBT) and the Nuclear Non-Proliferation Treaty (NPT) have emerged as the main points of India's participation with the international nuclear system. This sophisticated approach to nuclear diplomacy was evident in India's decision not to sign the Non-Proliferation Treaty (NPT) and its advocacy for disarmament while also keeping its nuclear weapons.

Regarding the Indo-American Civil Nuclear Agreement:

An important turning point in India's nuclear diplomacy occurred in 2008 when the United States and India signed the Indo-American Civil Nuclear Agreement. As a result of the agreement, India was effectively recognized as a responsible nuclear state, and civilian nuclear cooperation between India and the United States was made possible.

The deal marked a break from India's previous policy of nuclear isolation and highlighted the country's willingness to cooperate with the global non-proliferation framework on its own terms. There was a further elevation of India's worldwide position as a result of the strategic partnership that was formed with the United States.

Leadership on a Global Scale and Multilateral Engagements:

Aspirations of the United Nations Security Council (UNSC):

One of the recurring themes in India's diplomatic efforts has been the country's desire to secure a permanent seat on the United Nations Security Council (UNSC). In order to better reflect the geopolitical realities of the present day, India has been working to increase its presence on the United Nations Security Council. India is a key contributor to United Nations peacekeeping missions and a proponent of global governance reforms.

The aim of India to play a more prominent role in influencing international security and decision-making is reflected in the country's pursuit of membership in the United Nations Security Council. India's candidature continues to be a focal feature of its diplomatic efforts, despite the fact that progress on this front is being hampered by difficult circumstances.

Climate Change and the Leadership of the Global Environmental Community:

Because of its participation in international efforts to combat climate change, India has established itself as a responsible actor in matters pertaining to the environment. The nation's dedication to sustainable development, attempts to promote renewable energy, and participation in international climate change conferences are all examples of the country's leadership in the battle against climate change on a worldwide scale.

India has made considerable promises to decrease carbon emissions and transition to a more sustainable and green economy as a result of the Paris Agreement, which was ratified in 2015. These kinds of measures have helped to establish India's reputation as a responsible global player accountable for addressing crucial concerns.

The following are the challenges and ongoing considerations:

Regarding Diplomacy and Conflicts in the Region:

The issues that India has in the realm of diplomacy include the management of regional disputes and the maintenance of stability in its immediate area. For the sake of maintaining peace and stability in the area, it is necessary to employ nuanced diplomatic techniques in order to address issues such as the Kashmir conflict with Pakistan and border concerns with China.

The application of diplomatic strategies that are successful in resolving problems in the region not only adds to India's security but also to the country's standing in the international community. The maintenance of India's positive image on the international stage requires that ongoing efforts be made to find diplomatic solutions to problems that are occurring in the region.

The expansion of the economy and its impact on the world:

The respect that India receives on the international stage is directly related to both the country's economic progress and its involvement in the global economy. India's economic trajectory has ramifications for its ability to drive global economic policy and its influence in international forums. India is one of the main economies that is developing at the quickest rate in the globe.

In order for India to keep and improve its place on the international stage, it will be essential for the country to address difficulties relating to economic inequities, the development of infrastructure, and the promotion of innovation.

Strategic Alliances and the Dynamics of Geopolitical Situations:

Indian diplomatic concerns are shaped by the ever-changing geopolitical dynamics, notably those that are taking place in the Indo-Pacific area. Important features of India's global positioning include the formation and maintenance of strategic alliances with key players, the management of relations with significant countries, and the contribution to the stability of the area.

In order to achieve a state of equilibrium in its interactions with nations such as the United States of America, Russia, China, and other regional partners, it is necessary to navigate the geopolitical difficulties with great care.

From the pre-independence battle for self-rule to the present-day problems of a constantly changing global scene, the analysis of how "India" achieved worldwide recognition reveals a varied diplomatic journey that encompasses the whole spectrum of the country's history. The devotion of India's diplomatic efforts to concepts such as non-alignment, peace, and cooperation has resonated with governments all over the world. These principles have been a defining characteristic of India's diplomatic operations.

India's international prominence has progressively increased over the years, as seen by its successful pursuit of membership in the United Nations, its active participation in global forums, its resolution of regional crises, and its contributions to topics of global concern. Despite the fact that challenges continue to exist, India's diplomatic agenda is shaped by continuous considerations relating to economic growth, regional stability, and geopolitical factors.

It is expected that India's diplomatic contacts will continue to be an important component in determining its place on the world scene. This is because India continues to play a significant role in molding the future of the international community. Throughout its diplomatic journey, India has adhered to the ideals of peace, cooperation, and inclusivity. It is quite likely that these ideas will continue to serve as the foundation of India's approach to international relations in the years to come.

7.3 Reflection on the ongoing dialogue about identity and nomenclature in modern India

The continuous discourse concerning identity and nomenclature in contemporary India is a conversation that is dynamic and nuanced, reflecting the complexity of a nation that is both diverse and fast expanding. As India navigates the 21st century, questions about identity, cultural legacy, and nomenclature have gained significance, contributing to a nuanced analysis of the nation's sense of self. Specifically, several questions have been brought to the forefront. The purpose of this meditation is to delve into important facets of the ongoing conversation by analyzing the ways in which historical legacies, contemporary difficulties, and varied views impact the discourse on identity and nomenclature in contemporary India.

The historical foundations:

There is a continuous conversation taking place in modern India regarding identity and nomenclature, and its foundations are deeply established in the historical trajectory of the nation. Indelible marks have been left on the collective consciousness of the people as a result of the struggles for independence, the partition of the Indian subcontinent in 1947, and the subsequent process of nation-building that followed.

A commitment to historical continuity and a pan-Indian identity that transcended language and regional affinities was emphasized by the use of the name "India" as the official designation for the nation that had recently gained its independence. The Constitution of India, which was established in 1950, further represented a delicate balance by adopting both "India" and "Bharat" as names for the nation. This was done in recognition of the rich tapestry of historical and cultural identities that existed inside India.

The Diversity of Linguistic and Cultural Expressions:

The diversity of India's languages and cultures is one of the primary topics that are being discussed in the ongoing conversation. There are a great number of languages spoken in this country, each of which has its own writing system, literary traditions, and cultural peculiarities. Not only does this diversity provide a source of richness, but it also presents a problem when it comes to developing a national identity that is cohesive.

A pragmatic response to the linguistic diversity that existed at the time was the linguistic restructuring of states that took place in the 1950s and 1960s with the intention of achieving language homogeneity within states. The ongoing conversation, on the other hand, struggles with striking a careful balance between building a sense of national unity and supporting linguistic identities. A dedication to linguistic variety is reflected in the Eighth Schedule of the Constitution, which recognizes many languages as valid forms of communication.

Symbols and the Heritage of various cultures:

The continuous conversation regarding identity in modern India is significantly influenced by the cultural history and symbols that are present in the country. For the sake of preserving a link with India's illustrious history, it is believed that it is essential to preserve and promote cultural icons, historical sites, and traditional traditions.

In spite of this, there is the potential for disagreement about the meaning and depiction of cultural symbols. The dynamic aspect of the continuous discussion is highlighted by the debates that take place over the historical narratives of iconic persons, the renaming of towns, and the interpretation of historical events. Discussions on reinterpreting historical narratives in order to represent a more comprehensive understanding of India's past have arisen as a result of the assertion of cultural authenticity, which has been mixed with a desire for inclusivity.

Regional Identities and Federalism:

The federal structure of India, in which individual states have a significant amount of autonomy, is a factor that contributes to the continuous conversation regarding identity. Many of India's states have distinct regional identities that are rooted in their respective languages, histories, and cultures. One of the recurring themes is the conflict that arises between the aspirations of the region and the identity of the nation.

Efforts to promote regional languages, the celebration of regional festivals, and calls for greater autonomy are all essential components of the ongoing discourse. The delicate problem of striking a balance between nurturing regional identities and sustaining a cohesive national fabric continues to be a difficulty that highlights the inherent complexity that are present in India's federal structure.

The Impact of Globalization and Cultural Considerations:

Globalization has introduced new aspects to the ongoing conversation about identity in contemporary India, which has been going on for quite some time. A globalized Indian identity has emerged as a result of increased connectedness, exposure to global media, and the flow of ideas across boundaries. These factors have contributed to the mixing of cultures and the formation of those cultures.

Additionally, globalization raises concerns about the dissolution of traditional identities, despite the fact that it presents chances for cultural interchange and creativity. The current conversation is grappling with the impact that globalization has had on the cultural authenticity of India. This calls for a balanced approach to the preservation of traditional values while simultaneously accepting global influences.

The shifting demographics and the perspectives of young people:

A major portion of India's population is young people, which is a demographic factor that contributes to the continuous conversation over identity. It is not uncommon for the younger generation to have different goals, values, and points of view compared to the generation that came before them. Participants who are actively involved in developing the discourse on identity and nomenclature are the younger generation, which is marked by a global vision.

Young people now have the ability to engage in talks about identity in ways that were not available in the past because of the advent of social media as a platform for speech and action. Concerns such as language preferences, cultural representations, and modern difficulties are pushed to the forefront by the younger generation, which adds new aspects to the conversation that is now taking place.

Discussions Concerning Naming and Renaming:

The debates that are taking place over the name and renaming of cities, streets, and monuments are going to be one of the main points of the ongoing conversation. Discussions on representation, diversity, and historical authenticity have been sparked as a result of the reevaluation of names that are associated with colonial legacies, historical figures, and symbols.

The continuous conversation includes efforts to reclaim indigenous names, restore historical authenticity, and address the legacy of colonization. These are all included in the conversation. On the other hand, these discussions frequently give rise to contrasting points of view, with some individuals putting an emphasis on maintaining continuity with historical nomenclature while others advocate for alterations that are in line with contemporary norms.

Constitutional Framework and Inclusivity:

A solid foundation for resolving the challenges of identity in a nation that is ethnically and culturally diverse is provided by the Constitution of India. In the language of the constitution, the ideals of secularism, equality, and inclusivity are established, providing a foundation for the ongoing discourse that is taking place.

A vision of India that accepts variety within a democratic framework is something that may be attributed to the constitutional recognition of many languages, the right to retain and promote one's own culture, and the dedication to social justice. A number of ways in which the ongoing conversation is a reflection of the constitutional objectives that attempt to strike a balance between unity and diversity are present.

Prospective Courses of Action:

As India moves farther into the 21st century, it is likely that the ongoing conversation about identity and nomenclature will develop in response to new difficulties and opportunities that come up. The trajectory that the nation will take in the international arena will be determined by its capacity to handle the difficulties of identity while simultaneously cultivating a feeling of oneness.

The continuous conversation offers a forum for self-reflection, discussion, and the process of adjusting to shifting environmental conditions. This highlights the importance of adopting an approach that is inclusive, which recognizes the existence of a variety of perspectives, appreciates the existence of cultural plurality, and encourages a sense of common belonging among all residents.

A dynamic and crucial component of the development of the nation is the continuing conversation that is taking place in modern India regarding identity and nomenclature. Due to the fact that it is rooted in historical legacies, sculpted by cultural variety, and affected by modern challenges, the discourse reflects the intricacies of a nation that is always redefining itself.

The capacity to handle the continuing discourse with attention to linguistic diversity, cultural legacy, regional aspirations, and global influences will determine whether or not India is successful in forging a national identity that is coherent and inclusive. The continuous debate acts as a testament to the tenacity of India's democratic character, offering a space for many voices to contribute to the development of a nation that embraces both its rich legacy and its vibrant future. This was accomplished by creating a space for the dialogue to continue.

www.ingramcontent.com/pod-product-compliance
Lightning Source LLC
LaVergne TN
LVHW050648200726
843506LV00010B/1415